I0088991

Manifestation Plan

MANIFESTATION PLAN

Kenneth Walley

CIBUNET
Publishing

Manifestation Plan

Copyright © 2017 by Kenneth Walley

Manifestation Plan
By Kenneth Walley

Printed in the United States of America

ISBN: 10: 1-940260-00-0
ISBN: 13: 978-1-940260-00-6

All rights reserved. No part of this book may be reproduced, stored in retrieval system, or transmitted in any form or by any means: electronic, mechanical, photocopies, recording, scanning or other-except for brief quotations in critical reviews or articles, without the prior written permission of the publisher. This book or parts thereof may not be reproduced in any form, stored in a retrieval system, or transmitted in any form by any means- electronic, mechanical, photocopy, recording, or otherwise- without prior written permission of the publisher, except as provided by the United States of America copyright law. Unless otherwise noted, all Scripture quotations are from the New King James version of the Bible. Copyright © 1979, 1980, 1982 by Thomas Nelson, Inc., publishers Used by permission.

Published by
Cibunet Publishing
P. O. Box 444
Woodlawn, NY 10470
Email: admin@cibunet.com
Website: www.cibunet.com

TABLE OF CONTENTS

CHAPTER THREE
POST-MANIFESTATION ERA...93

INTRODUCTION

"What is it that you are building out there? Take it down and build it properly"

I woke up with this impression on my heart from a divine encounter one early morning, several years ago. I had recently started out in ministry and had engaged a contractor to build an office on my dad's property. I opted for the cheapest way to get the project done and as at this point, the walls were raised up almost to the roofing level. In the divine encounter, God revealed that there was a natural water way running through the land, and the office building project was in its path. When the contractor came in that morning with the construction crew, I had terrible news for them. Neighbors who had observed the progress of the building were all astonished when they saw the demolition in progress.

It was not long after we had rebuilt the project with reinforced foundations that a very heavy down pour of rain unveiled the natural waterway that would have destroyed the previous building had we gone through with it. Though personally it was a traumatic experience, I have learned throughout scripture that God always takes down what looks like a failure and starts over. A typical example is during the lifetime of Noah; God destroyed all creatures through a flood and started afresh with those who were preserved by the Noah's ark.

The common midlife story for many people on earth today is often that of shattered aspirations, broken dreams and hope deferred. Our human nature, endowments, community, natural resources, fault lines and creator altogether constitute the design of how we prosper in life. Developing an insightful relationship with the visible and invisible world around us is the key to a meaningful, fulfilling and enduring impact.

The story of Joseph in the scriptures unveils his unique insights by which he made a significant impact on his world as well as the inevitable transitions that most people have to go through from divine promise to physical manifestation. These three phases of transition in Joseph's life were: the Pre-Manifestation era of his life that is prior to his appointment to the palace, the Manifestation period when Joseph became Prime Minister and Egypt experienced abundance for seven years and the Post-Manifestation era characterized by seven years of drought. We find several examples of this pattern in the scriptures that paint a similar picture:

Abraham is promised that his biological offspring will become a great nation, but then he goes through the process of time before Isaac his son of promise is born and ultimately the fullness of the promise become a reality.

Israel as a slave nation in Egypt is promised the Land of Canaan, but then they go through the plagues in Egypt and a wilderness experience before they finally possess the Promised Land.

King David is anointed king over Israel as a teenager but then he goes through a period of persecution from King Saul before his ultimate coronation as king of Israel.

While we go through the wilderness experience of our calling and destiny, the first question is: what should we be doing in preparation? The scripture tells us that Israel was delayed in the wilderness for forty years when they could have possessed the Promised Land after a forty day journey. An entire generation died on the way not being able to inherit the promises of God so it was their offspring that possessed the Promised Land.

After conquering territories in the Promised Land, some Israelite communities were unable to hold on to their inheritance and remained victims of oppression from their heathen neighbors. The question here is: how do we conduct ourselves in order to hold on to our blessings?

In the story of Joseph, we see his influence extended beyond the borders of Egypt as people from several nations were impacted by the wisdom of God evident in his life. The question here is: how do we enlarge our coasts and expand our influence when we come into our season of prosperity and God makes a way?

Manifestation Plan

Chapter
One

PRE-MANIFESTATION ERA

"I am Alpha and Omega, the beginning and the ending, saith the Lord, which is, and which was, and which is to come, the Almighty" Revelation 1:8.

At the age of seventeen, Joseph had a dream, in which he was with his brothers binding sheaves of grain out in the field. Suddenly his sheaf rose and stood upright, while their sheaves gathered around his and bowed down to it. Joseph had a second dream around this time in which the sun and moon and eleven stars were bowing down to him. When he told his father as well as his brothers, his father rebuked him and said, "What is this dream you had? Will your mother and I and your brothers actually come and bow down to the ground before you?" His brothers were jealous of him, but his father kept the matter in mind.

Assuming you have a promise from God through prophetic revelation or visions or dreams which have not yet been fulfilled, then this period of your life is known as pre-manifestation. God furnishes us with a unique environment so we can make preparations that set the stage for the manifestation of his promises. To begin preparing, we have to identify the entities in our immediate world. In his message to the Greeks who were listening to him on Mars Hill in Athens, the Apostle Paul describes God as the one who determines our world at every point in time.

"God that made the world and all things therein, seeing that he is Lord of heaven and earth, dwelleth not in temples made with hands; Neither is worshipped with men's hands, as though he needed any thing, seeing he giveth to all life, and breath, and all things; And hath made of one blood all nations of men for to dwell on all the face of the earth, and hath determined the times before appointed, and the bounds of their habitation; That they should seek the Lord, if haply they might feel after him, and find him, though he be not far from every one of us: For in him we live, and move, and have our being; as certain also of your own poets have said, For we are also his offspring" Acts 17:24-28.

At every point in time, God surrounds every human being with people, entities and resources that have a role to play in their destiny. It is a function of His Sovereign design. It is our responsibility to identify and profile these people and resources to determine how to harness them for our utmost benefit. "For by him were all things created, that are in heaven, and that are in earth, visible and invisible, whether they be thrones, or dominions, or principalities, or powers: all things were created by him, and for him: And he is before all things, and by him all things consist. And he is the head of the body, the church: who is the beginning, the firstborn from the dead; that in all things he might have the preeminence" Colossians 1:16-18.

Here in this scripture, the Apostle Paul sheds light on the divine attribute by which we are all surrounded by entities and resources that are intended to furnish our divine destiny. We must never be ignorant of what is placed in our world by divine design. In the book of Revelations chapter one, while banished at the Island of Patmos the Apostle John received a visitation from Jesus Christ. This is a breakdown of what Jesus told John:

- I am Alpha - The Beginning - Purpose
- I am Omega - The Ending - Destiny
- Which Was - The Past - Knowledge
- Which Is - The Present - Understanding
- Which Is To Come - The Future - Wisdom

THE PAST, PRESENT AND FUTURE

During the Pre-Manifestation era of Joseph's life in Egypt, we see how God surrounds his life with three people: "And it came to pass after these things, that the butler of the king of Egypt and his baker had offended their lord the king of Egypt. And Pharaoh was wroth against two of his officers, against the chief

of the butlers, and against the chief of the bakers. And
he put them in ward in the house of the captain of the
guard, into the prison, the place where Joseph was
bound. And the captain of the guard charged Joseph
with them, and he served them: and they continued a
season in ward. And they dreamed a dream both of
them, each man his dream in one night, each man
according to the interpretation of his dream, the
butler and the baker of the king of Egypt, which were
bound in the prison. And Joseph came in unto them
in the morning, and looked upon them, and, behold,
they were sad. And he asked Pharaoh's officers that
were with him in the ward of his lord's house, saying,
Wherefore look ye so sadly today? And they said unto
him, We have dreamed a dream, and there is no
interpreter of it. And Joseph said unto them, Do not
interpretations belong to God? tell me them, I pray
you. And the chief butler told his dream to Joseph,
and said to him, In my dream, behold, a vine was
before me; And in the vine were three branches: and
it was as though it budded, and her blossoms shot
forth; and the clusters thereof brought forth ripe
grapes: And Pharaoh's cup was in my hand: and I
took the grapes, and pressed them into Pharaoh's cup,
and I gave the cup into Pharaoh's hand. And Joseph
said unto him, This is the interpretation of it: The
three branches are three days: Yet within three days
shall Pharaoh lift up thine head, and restore thee unto
thy place: and thou shalt deliver Pharaoh's cup into
his hand, after the former manner when thou wast his

butler. But think on me when it shall be well with thee, and shew kindness, I pray thee, unto me, and make mention of me unto Pharaoh, and bring me out of this house: For indeed I was stolen away out of the land of the Hebrews: and here also have I done nothing that they should put me into the dungeon. When the chief baker saw that the interpretation was good, he said unto Joseph, I also was in my dream, and, behold, I had three white baskets on my head: And in the uppermost basket there was of all manner of bakemeats for Pharaoh; and the birds did eat them out of the basket upon my head. And Joseph answered and said, This is the interpretation thereof: The three baskets are three days: Yet within three days shall Pharaoh lift up thy head from off thee, and shall hang thee on a tree; and the birds shall eat thy flesh from off thee. And it came to pass the third day, which was Pharaoh's birthday, that he made a feast unto all his servants: and he lifted up the head of the chief butler and of the chief baker among his servants. And he restored the chief butler unto his butlership again; and he gave the cup into Pharaoh's hand: But he hanged the chief baker: as Joseph had interpreted to them. Yet did not the chief butler remember Joseph, but forgat him" Genesis 40.

Here we see the Captain of the Guard, the Chief Baker and Chief Butler are three people who play a significant role in Joseph's life just preceding his position as Prime Minister of Egypt.

The Captain of the Guard represents the Present Condition of Joseph. The Captain of the Guard gave Joseph an assignment of Chief Operating Officer because he was aware that Joseph had served Potiphar as Chief Executive Officer. When Joseph was placed in charge of Potiphar's estate, it is recorded that Potiphar's estate prospered exceedingly. It is possible that Potiphar's estate became the leading enterprise in Egypt so everyone was aware of Joseph's exceptional leadership skills. By placing all that took place in the Prison Facility under the care of Joseph, the Captain of the Guard put Joseph's skills to work.

He had a working relationship with Joseph and so we can refer to him as Joseph's boss or employer in the light of this assignment. The Chief Baker was brought into the Prison where Joseph was serving because he had offended the Pharaoh. As a top government official of the Pharaoh, he was considered a high profile prisoner and the Captain of the Guard placed him directly under the care of Joseph. As his vocation indicates, the Chief Baker was responsible for the Food Production of Egypt. Food is responsible for our growth and physiological development. When we look at the physical appearance of a healthy thirty-year old person, what we see is the history of food that this fellow has consumed over thirty years of existence on earth. If we engage such a person in a lengthy conversation we may be able to tell their level of education and to some extent, their intellectual capacity. The Chief Baker is significant of Joseph's past. The reason he is in prison with Joseph is the divine assignment to reinforce Joseph's foundations. There are people who God places in our world to establish or reinforce a solid foundation in our lives.

Sometimes it is difficult to appreciate such people because they consistently challenge us to study, take up higher education and increase our learning. Once we can earn a decent income from our professional training, it is natural for most of us to become complacent with our level of education and professional achievement which makes us plateau in wisdom. However for the dimension of manifestation that God has in mind for His people, it requires the best and most solid of all foundations. God's ultimate design is for us to be the "head and not the tail, above only and never beneath". As a young boy I attended high school and lived in a boarding house and so I often communicated with my dad through letters. In all of his letters my dad will quote this scripture from 2 Timothy 2:15, "Study to shew thyself approved unto God, a workman that needeth not to be ashamed, rightly dividing the word of truth." As a young boy in boarding school I always wanted extra money for delicacies and treats for my 'sweet tooth' and so I will often times be irritated by this quote especially if the letter did not come with money enclosed. Eventually I found myself using the same quote anytime I wrote a letter to my older brother Benny who was working on a ship. I would often encourage him to take time off work to seek further training in Engineering which was his field. As would many people, he got offended at this quote which was now appearing in all my mails and protested so I stopped.

The Chief Baker's dream also throws light into what he represented in the scheme of Joseph's destiny. He dreamt that there were three white baskets of bake meats on his head but the birds came and ate these bake meats from the baskets. Joseph interpreted that in three days the Chief Baker will be executed by Pharaoh, which happened exactly as Joseph interpreted. The Chief Baker had completed his assignment to the Pharaoh and his last assignment in life was to reinforce Joseph's foundation in preparation for the position of Prime Minister.

The Chief Butler was in charge of the Beverage Industry in Egypt. Beverages make our heart glad. This is significant of inspiration. What inspires us mostly is information that promises a better tomorrow. The Chief Butler had a dream that speaks to his function in Joseph's life in Prison. He dreamt that he was serving Pharaoh with wine from fruits. Joseph interprets that the Chief Butler would be restored to his office with the Pharaoh and this happened exactly as predicted. Joseph gave the Chief Butler an assignment to mention him to the Pharaoh when he is restored to his position. The Chief Butler clearly represents Joseph's future.

Within the context of time, we are three-dimensional beings and as Jesus said to John, He manifests as our past, present and future to furnish us to His glory.

"I AM HE WHICH WAS"

The Lord Jesus Christ places people in our world who represent our past. Such people have the responsibility of establishing and reinforcing our foundations. As humans we are Spirit, have a Soul and live in a Body. With our Spirit, we have a relationship with God and serve in a priestly or spiritual capacity at Church. With our Soul we have a relationship with our family and friends so we relate to them in an emotional or prophetic capacity. With our Body we have a relationship with the earth where we are called as kings, and so we are involved in a vocation by which we earn finances.

In every aspect of our lives, we all desire to flourish and become accomplished. To become accomplished and prosperous we need to have solid foundations. Within the framework of the Church, we have Bible Teachers whose function is to equip us with solid spiritual foundations. In our social community we have elderly and experienced people who help us build our emotional foundations so that we can thrive in our family relationships. In our careers and professional vocation, we have professors and trained teachers who equip us at school with skill to become competent in our work.

It is important that we develop an ear for such people whose discourse with us, often challenge us to take steps that ultimately strengthen our foundations. Such people encourage us to operate in the Spirit of Excellence because that is their natural burden for us. To embrace their counsel is how we guarantee that tomorrow will be better than today. Most often how we are appreciated today is indicative of the kind of foundation we built in our past. We would never be appreciated beyond our fundamental capacity. If we feel unappreciated or underappreciated today, then we should be paying attention to our teachers, seek more training or go back to school and reinforce our foundations.

"I AM, WHICH IS"

In His visitation to the Apostle John, Jesus Christ said: "I Am Which Is." This is reference to our present time. In His Sovereignty, God surrounds our lives with people such as employers, employees, a Pastor, family relatives, friends, acquaintances as well as all those who make our life currently comfortable. If we are constantly in conflict with such people then our lives become miserable because no one wants to have any dealings with us. Those in our world today have a giving and receiving relationship with us. How much we are willing to give, determines what we receive from them. If we give less we get less, if we give more we also get more.

"I AM WHICH IS TO COME"

Jesus described Himself to the Apostle John as being the "One Which Is To Come." Jesus Christ is indeed our future. He holds the key to our tomorrow and so He surrounds us with people who carry that burden. They are those who spur us to save money, make an investment or even start an enterprise. Spiritually these are the Apostles and Prophets at Church. Financially these are our Investment Advisors, Financial Planners or Accountants. Socially these are elderly people who encourage us to marry or stay married to keep the family intact.

It is so sad to see so many people remain static and actually retrogress as they grow older in life. You look at such people and it seems as though time had a negative impact on their lives and well-being. Retrogression should never be the picture of a man's life. To enjoy a progressive life, our decision-making must always reflect who we are as three-dimensional beings, so that adequate resources are invested to reinforce our past (foundations), give to those who represent our present (current relationships) and invest against tomorrow (the future).

"I AM ALPHA"

Alpha means the beginning. This is how Jesus inserts purpose into our being. We are enabled by the nature of God to function in our divine potentials according to God's master plan for our lives. It all starts with accepting who we are in the eyes of God. Jeremiah's calling is a classical instance in the scriptures:

"Then the word of the LORD came unto me, saying, Before I formed thee in the belly I knew thee; and before thou camest forth out of the womb I sanctified thee, and I ordained thee a prophet unto the nations. Then said I, Ah, Lord GOD! behold, I cannot speak: for I am a child. But the LORD said unto me, Say not, I am a child: for thou shalt go to all that I shall send thee, and whatsoever I command thee thou shalt speak. Be not afraid of their faces: for I am with thee to deliver thee, saith the LORD. Then the LORD put forth his hand, and touched my mouth. And the LORD said unto me, Behold, I have put my words in thy mouth. See, I have this day set thee over the nations and over the kingdoms, to root out, and to pull down, and to destroy, and to throw down, to build, and to plant" Jeremiah 1:4-10.

As famous as Jeremiah eventually became as a Prophet in Israel, you will notice that this dialogue is a preliminary encounter between God and Jeremiah. For the first time, Jeremiah becomes aware that he is a Prophet. His reaction is somehow shocking: "I cannot speak, I am a child." In those days a Prophet was thought of as having a typical profile that Jeremiah did not possess as a young man. Prophets had a unique manner of accent when speaking a "Thus saith the Lord" that made the listener feel as though God himself was talking. Also Prophets were usually old people with probably a sophisticated gray mustache.

God answered Jeremiah's protest directly: "Say not, I am a child: for thou shalt go to all that I shall send thee, and whatsoever I command thee thou shalt speak." The plans of God for our lives are not intended to fit into what society may have become as a result of the degenerate ways of people under the influence of the kingdom of darkness. God's plans for our lives were determined long before we were born into this world. If only we would yield to function in the divine call, this is how God gets to insert Himself into the framework of our existence to manifest His good intentions to our generation.

In the light of the reality of potential opposition to the mission, He assured Jeremiah "Be not afraid of their faces: for I am with thee to deliver thee." Established institutions and personalities within a particular generation will oftentimes resist strongly, any new-comer that resembles a formidable competition or threat to their existence.

The revelation of God as Alpha comes out clearly in how He intends to be present with Jeremiah both to fulfill the mission as well as defend him against any form of intimidation or adversity. Furthermore, God enhances Jeremiah's human nature by touching Jeremiah's mouth. "Then the LORD put forth his hand, and touched my mouth. And the LORD said unto me, Behold, I have put my words in thy mouth." Remember when God called Moses in the burning bush encounter, He enhanced Moses' rod and body for signs and wonders. He does the same with Jeremiah and then gives scope to Jeremiah's mission: "See, I have this day set thee over the nations and over the kingdoms, to root out, and to pull down, and to destroy, and to throw down, to build, and to plant." This is the ultimate scope of Jeremiah's mission that is, over the nations and kingdoms.

The nations here signify individuals while kingdoms signify institutions or organizations. The dynamics of the assignment is first of all to root out, pull down, destroy and throw down. This four-fold termination phase of his assignment was targeted at the superstructure of any demonic system. In Deuteronomy 7:5, Moses had taught the Israelites how to deal with demonic strongholds when they took possession of any new territory in the Promised Land: "But thus shall ye deal with them; ye shall destroy their altars, and break down their images, and cut down their groves, and burn their graven images with fire." The kingdom of darkness is structured to comprise of a spiritual system made up of images, a grove, an altar and an idol. When this four part system is in place; Dominion Spirits, Powers, Principalities and Satan are invoked to reign over a space or territory. In every place where Jeremiah would be assigned, God expected that he would primarily destroy the demonic system in place before attempting to establishing kingdom structures that is to 'build and plant.'

Though these instructions are to Jeremiah, they teach us the fundamentals of any divine assignment. They were written for our learning so that God does not have to repeat them every time He gives us an assignment. God manifests as Alpha to the world, whenever we yield ourselves to answer our calling to fulfill our divine assignment.

"I AM OMEGA"

Omega means ending. The end gives the sense of destiny. Jesus was telling the Apostle John that He was divine destiny. Anything that starts with Him also ends in Him. In the discourse with Jeremiah, God unfolds this truth: "Moreover the word of the LORD came unto me, saying, Jeremiah, what seest thou? And I said, I see a rod of an almond tree. Then said the LORD unto me, Thou hast well seen: for I will hasten my word to perform it" Jeremiah 1:11&12.

In this vision, He shows Jeremiah the rod of all almond tree. Once he ascertains that Jeremiah has caught a glimpse of the revelation, He explains the meaning: "I will hasten my word to perform it." In other words, 'I am watching over my words to perform it.' God is assuring Jeremiah that He will not delay in manifesting as Omega if only Jeremiah will avail himself to fulfill his assignment. Omega is the exclusive role of God within the scheme of our divine assignment. That is how He shows up to meet us at the point of our needs, as a deliverer in times of trouble, as answers in our hearts when posed with difficult questions, as creative solutions when faced with walls of limitations.

He has promised to insert Himself into our lives and equip us as Alpha if only we yield ourselves. Each time we take a step in fulfillment of our divine assignment, He assures us that He will not delay to match our steps as Omega. He is watching over His Word to perform it. What an awesome commitment from the Almighty!

"A BOILING POT"

I assume that Jeremiah is excited after this divine encounter and is brooding over all that God has told him then suddenly God shows up again!
"And the word of the LORD came unto me the second time, saying, What seest thou? And I said, I see a seething pot; and the face thereof is toward the north. Then the LORD said unto me, Out of the north an evil shall break forth upon all the inhabitants of the land. For, lo, I will call all the families of the kingdoms of the north, saith the LORD; and they shall come, and they shall set every one his throne at the entering of the gates of Jerusalem, and against all the walls thereof round about, and against all the cities of Judah. And I will utter my judgments against them touching all their wickedness, who have forsaken me, and have burned incense unto other gods, and worshipped the works of their own hands. Thou

therefore gird up thy loins, and arise, and speak unto them all that I command thee: be not dismayed at their faces, lest I confound thee before them. For, behold, I have made thee this day a defenced city, and an iron pillar, and brasen walls against the whole land, against the kings of Judah, against the princes thereof, against the priests thereof, and against the people of the land. And they shall fight against thee; but they shall not prevail against thee; for I am with thee, saith the LORD, to deliver thee" Jeremiah 1:13-19.

Hmmmmnn... A boiling pot! Why! This is the reaction of the enemy to God's intentions with Jeremiah. The enemy reigns on this earth through his influence on mainstream human culture. As long as he has a handle on those at the helm of affairs in our governments and institutions, his reign remains solid. Now however, there seems to be a new Mayor in town who has been commissioned by the Almighty God to undertake an assignment that undermines the devil's reign here on earth. The devil is incensed. He is angry and boiling! God's commissioning of Jeremiah to destroy the system by which he manipulates the earth does not sit well with him. IT IS TIME FOR WAR!

He will deploy all his forces to target the walls and gates of Jerusalem. He will also try to incite adversity from within the government of Israel and the Priesthood. That is the stock-in-trade of the enemy. He works both from within and without so that we start to doubt our divine calling. The enemy knows that whenever those you thought of as friends turn into enemies, your confidence usually tends to collapse. This is why he works to influence your friends against you as a part of his overall scheme. God encourages Jeremiah not to give up his confidence in the face of any attack from opposition. "For, behold, I have made thee this day a defenced city, and an iron pillar, and brasen walls against the whole land." In other words, I have reinforced who you are in the face of all those who will come against you. God will always defends us, reinforce our elements with the strongest and most durable materials to resist any form of attack. No weapon forged against us shall prosper!

It was extremely important that Jeremiah should uphold his confidence in God during adversity. "And they shall fight against thee; but they shall not prevail against thee; for I am with thee, saith the LORD, to deliver thee." The outcome of any form of adversity is already set in stone. You will prevail regardless of the attack against you. This is the kind of confidence required in the pursuit of any divine assignment. God reinforces our ability to resist the devil. Angels are at our defense, they stand as a supernatural support of our pillars and walls on all sides.

FEASIBILITY DILIGENCE

In the pursuit of our divine calling and assignment, we must never be oblivious of the enemy.

Though God had promised Israel the Land of Canaan as a possession, he led Moses through some steps which are recorded in the scriptures for our due diligence. In Numbers 13, Moses selects the leaders of the twelve tribes of Israel to embark on a mission to spy out the Promised Land.

"And Moses sent them to spy out the land of Canaan, and said unto them, Get you up this way southward, and go up into the mountain: And see the land, what it is, and the people that dwelleth therein, whether they be strong or weak, few or many; And what the land is that they dwell in, whether it be good or bad; and what cities they be that they dwell in, whether in tents, or in strong holds; And what the land is, whether it be fat or lean, whether there be wood therein, or not" Numbers 13:17-20.

Today we call this act of spying - Feasibility Study. Moses commissioned these tribal leaders with six benchmarks by which they will report back to him. Though God had promised them the land of the Canaanites, it was important that they should have an overall knowledge of the potential resistance to their conquests. They needed fair insight as to how the current inhabitants of the Promised Land were positioned to resist their Assignment, People, Culture, Work, Reputation and Money. It is an important diligence to have a good grasp of these six areas where the enemy works actively to oppose any human endeavor that is contrary to his agenda.

ASSIGNMENT

"Whether there be wood therein, or not." This was a specific benchmark of Moses to the tribal leaders that was core to the overall assignment. Any place on earth where there is wood in abundance allows for much construction of edifices and development. Think of a forest and you quickly realize that as a prosperous ecosystem almost everything thrives. It is the natural sense of a city or community with thriving industrial activities. Moses wanted to know if the Promised Land comprised of mega corporations and big industrial entities. As much as this becomes intimidating to overcome, it is also indicative of the potentials of the land. Assuming there was much wood in the land, two things come into play which are: adequate logistical resourcefulness as well as psychological anticipation of great gain.

The enemy engages us in a psychological battle that is intended to cast doubt and fear in our minds concerning the overall pursuit of a divine assignment. The following is an example of a question that may bombard our minds as evidence of a psychological attack: Has God really called you to this mission or could it be the fragment of your own imagination?
The reason the enemy pushes such a question into our minds is to try and eliminate the God factor from the assignment. If God can be eliminated from the assignment, then we can size ourselves as ill-equipped to tackle the endeavor. So then, do not even try to pursue it. It is destined to fail! Think of all

the billion dollar corporations that are well established globally that you intend to compete against! Don't even try it, because they will crush your efforts, drown and bury you quickly! You immediately advise yourself that it a waste of time and resources trying to pursue a project that will ultimately fail so it is better to pull the breaks now before you get started!

The Prophet Habakkuk was confronted with the same situation where he was confronted with terrible times and a lot of psychological inhibition. This was his solution: "I will stand upon my watch, and set me upon the tower, and will watch to see what he will say unto me, and what I shall answer when I am reproved. And the LORD answered me, and said, Write the vision, and make it plain upon tables, that he may run that readeth it. For the vision is yet for an appointed time, but at the end it shall speak, and not lie: though it tarry, wait for it; because it will surely come, it will not tarry" Habakkuk 2:1-3.

"I will stand upon my watch" - This meant that he would walk in obedience to the basic commands of the scriptures he knew to keep himself compliant. "And set me upon the tower" - A tower was the projection of a city where soldiers will often stand to observe whatever was coming from far. This meant that he will intensify his prayers to God. "And what I shall answer when I am reproved" - The reprover here is the enemy. Habakkuk is in a constant mental battle with the enemy in regards to his calling. That is how the enemy has chosen to engage him. It is a psychological warfare. Habakkuk is seeking God for a "Thus saith Lord" by which he would rebuke the enemy that casts a doubt in his mind in regards to his calling and assignment. It can be very inhibiting when you are constantly in doubt as to if God has really called you to an assignment. It is crippling and sometimes holds you back from the pursuit of purpose over long periods of time.

This time around God answers Habakkuk with a solution that overcomes his constant psychological inhibition: "Write the vision, and make it plain upon tables, that he may run that readeth it." Put pen and paper to all that I will tell you. Wow! There is a saying that 'a short pencil is better than a big memory.' Habakkuk's psychological inhibition is simply because he never penned down his divine assignment. There was no point of reference for what God had told him so the enemy could always play tricks with his mind. Furthermore, God tells him to make it plain upon tables that he may run that reads it. This gives the sense of a well crafted plan that gives function to people who have a role to play in the mission. Also He tells Habakkuk an important truth.

"For the vision is yet for an appointed time, but at the end it shall speak, and not lie: though it tarry, wait for it; because it will surely come, it will not tarry." This speaks to the essence of objectivity in the plan. This is means that Habakkuk must incorporate what God does in every season as a feature of the plan. In essence God told Habakkuk that the way to overcome the challenge of doubting his calling and assignment was to craft a plan that has benchmarks and objectives.

PEOPLE

"Whether they be strong or weak." This benchmark that Moses required of the tribal leaders was to ascertain the human resource potentials of the Promised Land. Strong People are those who are highly skilled and competent professionally while weak people signify less skill and professional competence. We learnt earlier on about how that God surrounds us with people who have a role to play in our lives and within the scheme of our divine destiny. Such people facilitate us in several ways that make us dependent on them either directly or indirectly. If they come under attack from the enemy then we suffer somehow because they are unable to be the fullness of what they ought to be to us.

Assuming such people come under attack of the enemy, it is our responsibility to stand in the gap for them. "Therefore will I divide him a portion with the great, and he shall divide the spoil with the strong; because he hath poured out his soul unto death: and he was numbered with the transgressors; and he bare the sin of many, and made intercession for the transgressors" Isaiah 53:12.

Everyone who stands with us in the scheme of our divine assignment is a part of God's overall plan to prosper us. They deserve their portion of the blessings we enjoy from God such as peace of mind, health and provision. When they sin and fall short of the glory of God, we do not 'throw them under the bus.' Rather we pray for them and trust that God will forgive, heal and restore them. Our ministry to those who God has placed in our world is that of INTERCESSION!

CULTURE

"And what the land is that they dwell in, whether it be good or bad." This benchmark of Moses to the tribal leaders who went to spy out the Promised Land was to ascertain its cultural potentials. Good land is usually one that is endowed with valuable natural resources, such as gold, metals and also very suitable for farming or grazing cattle. The natural endowment of the land in a community has a relationship with those traditions that are upheld in such communities. In those days where the economies were typically agricultural and mining, the cultural influence as a prosperity benchmark was limited to the potentials of land itself. Today however, the cultural influence on the prosperity of a place will often be the lifestyle and practices of the people based on their overall philosophical inclinations. The Apostle Paul tells the Colossians:

"Beware lest any man spoil you through philosophy and vain deceit, after the tradition of men, after the rudiments of the world, and not after Christ. For in him dwelleth all the fulness of the Godhead bodily. And ye are complete in him, which is the head of all principality and power: In whom also ye are circumcised with the circumcision made without hands, in putting off the body of the sins of the flesh by the circumcision of Christ: Buried with him in baptism, wherein also ye are risen with him through the faith of the operation of God, who hath raised him from the dead. And you, being dead in your sins and the uncircumcision of your flesh, hath he quickened together with him, having forgiven you all trespasses; Blotting out the handwriting of ordinances that was against us, which was contrary to us, and took it out of the way, nailing it to his cross; And having spoiled principalities and powers, he made a shew of them openly, triumphing over them in it" Colossians 2:8-15.

One of the ways by which the enemy keeps a handle over a human community is to influence its culture. This way the enemy controls the people through their mindsets and thought patterns regardless of whether they worship him directly or not. In every society, there are those who directly lend themselves to demonic influence through the practice of divination and occult. There are others who do not serve Satan directly but then become open to whatever is considered a mainstream philosophy or traditions. Satan penetrates the fabric of our societies by advocating practices through his direct followers in very subtle ways that appeal to the simple minds of people in a community. Some of these traditions and philosophies are promoted by secular media and sometimes end up in books, in school curriculums, or social festivities marked as a public holiday.

If the Apostle Paul was addressing cultural backlashes in the scriptures, then it would not be wrong to assume that the Christians in Colossi were battling the enemy on this issue. He reassures them of the power of baptism. The fullness of the Godhead dwells in bodily form in Christ Jesus. We are complete in Jesus Christ who is the head of all principality and power. We have been forgiven all our sins. Through baptism we are dead in Christ and raised to life through the operation of God. The blood of Jesus has blotted out the handwriting of ordinances that was against us, which was contrary to us, and took it out of the way, nailing it to his cross; And having spoiled principalities and powers, he made a shew of them openly, triumphing over them in it. Baptism immerses us into the fullness of the Godhead. We have become one with Christ Jesus and so we cannot be bullied by people into accepting cultural practices that violate our divine convictions. Through baptism we are now a part of God's kingdom culture and have a divine mandate to actively push and establish godly practices to override demonic inspired cultures in our communities.

WORK

"Whether it be fat or lean." Fat or lean lands refer to the productivity potentials of a place. Moses required this benchmark as part of the report he expected from the tribal leaders who were going out to spy the Promised Land. At any point when people become complacent and refuse to increase their learning so as to increase their knowledge base, their productivity plateaus. The tribe of Ephraim was particularly blessed with great pasture lands as their possession and so they became trapped with the vice of pride. In Isaiah 28:1 the scripture says: "Woe to the crown of pride, to the drunkards of Ephraim, whose glorious beauty is a fading flower, which are on the head of the fat valleys of them that are overcome with wine!" The Ephraimites had become complacent in their ways and were no longer open to the counsel of God in their work. God describes them as a fading flower which meant that over time, they would diminish in prosperity. In this same scripture, God tells the process by which he makes us flourish in our work.

"Give ye ear, and hear my voice; hearken, and hear my speech. Doth the plowman plow all day to sow? doth he open and break the clods of his ground? When he hath made plain the face thereof, doth he not cast abroad the fitches, and scatter the cummin, and cast in the principal wheat and the appointed barley and the rie in their place? For his God doth instruct him to discretion, and doth teach him. For the fitches are not threshed with a threshing instrument, neither is a cart wheel turned about upon the cummin; but the fitches are beaten out with a staff, and the cummin with a rod. Bread corn is bruised; because he will not ever be threshing it, nor break it with the wheel of his cart, nor bruise it with his horsemen. This also cometh forth from the LORD of hosts, which is wonderful in counsel, and excellent in working" Isaiah 28:23-29.

God is the source of the inspiration by which a farmer uses the right tools to prepare soil as well as how to cultivate specific seeds in the appropriate kind of soil. He counsels the farmer to process the harvest in a spirit of excellence so that the results of the farmer's work turns out wonderful and appreciated by all. "But he giveth more grace. Wherefore he saith, God resisteth the proud, but giveth grace unto the humble" James 4:6. If only we would submit to the counsel of God, our work will turn out wonderful rewards.

REPUTATION

"Few or many." Moses requested the tribal leaders who were going to spy the Promised Land to check the market potential. Few people signify a weak market while many people are an indication of a big market. The number of those who patronize whatever we do determines how prosperous we become. Assuming you went into a market place with few people present, the chances of selling a lot of your goods or services becomes limited to those few who are present as opposed to when the number of people present is huge.

Since our prosperity is linked to the number of people who patronize us, the enemy may attempt to limit those who patronize our assignment by attacking our reputation. In Acts 13:6-12 we see a similar scenario: "And when they had gone through the isle unto Paphos, they found a certain sorcerer, a false prophet, a Jew, whose name was Barjesus: Which was with the deputy of the country, Sergius Paulus, a prudent man; who called for Barnabas and Saul, and desired to hear the word of God. But Elymas the sorcerer (for so is his name by interpretation) withstood them, seeking to turn away the deputy from the faith. Then Saul, (who also is called Paul,) filled with the Holy Ghost, set his eyes on him. And said, O full of all subtilty and all mischief, thou child of the devil, thou enemy of all righteousness, wilt thou not cease to pervert the right ways of the Lord? And now, behold, the hand of the Lord is upon thee, and thou shalt be blind, not seeing the sun for a season. And immediately there fell on him a mist and a darkness; and he went about seeking some to lead him by the hand. Then the deputy, when he saw what was done, believed, being astonished at the doctrine of the Lord."

There are three parties in this story. The Apostle Paul is the preacher who is spreading the gospel. The Deputy Sergius Paulus is the potential customer. The sorcerer BarJesus Elymas is an agent of the devil. In this plot the Apostle Paul is attempting to preach the gospel to the Deputy Sergius Paulus but then Elymas the sorcerer is casting doubts on the ministry of the Apostle Paul. Elymas is probably discounting the message of the Apostle Paul and making remarks that cast a shadow on the apostle's reputation. The Apostle Paul is experiencing a resistance that he is obviously unable to match with words so he resorts to the supernatural. He leverages his authority and unleashes blindness upon Elymas the sorcerer. When the declaration of blindness pronounced by Paul happens, the Deputy Sergius Paulus encounters the efficacy of the power of God and believes in the gospel.

In the great commission to all believers to spread the gospel Jesus told the disciples: "And he said unto them, Go ye into all the world, and preach the gospel to every creature. He that believeth and is baptized shall be saved; but he that believeth not shall be damned. And these signs shall follow them that believe; In my name shall they cast out devils; they shall speak with new tongues; They shall take up serpents; and if they drink any deadly thing, it shall not hurt them; they shall lay hands on the sick, and they shall recover. So then after the Lord had spoken unto them, he was received up into heaven, and sat on the right hand of God. And they went forth, and preached everywhere, the Lord working with them, and confirming the word with signs following. Amen" Mark 16:15-20.

As believers we have been given the authority for signs and wonders to validate the gospel. This is exactly what the Apostle Paul did to authenticate the gospel when he experienced the resistance of Elymas. The overall impact of this wonder was that the Deputy Sergius Paulus received salvation after the demonstration of the power of God.

In pursuit of our divine assignment, we are endowed with divine authority to leverage signs and wonders especially when our reputation is under attack. Signs and wonders will always validate the authenticity of Christ in our lives.

MONEY

"What cities they be that they dwell in, whether in tents, or in strong holds." Tents or strongholds tell of the level of wealth in a place. Where there is little treasure, the owners dwell in tents but then when people build up large amounts of treasure they only feel secure in stronghold cities. This is an important benchmark for any venture or assignment and Moses required the tribal leaders to ascertain this.

Usually the enemy devices an attack against our traditional sources of revenue. When this happens we are pushed up against a wall in the face of our financial obligations. The Apostle Paul talks to the Philippians about how to overcome this: "Now ye Philippians know also, that in the beginning of the gospel, when I departed from Macedonia, no church communicated with me as concerning giving and receiving, but ye only. For even in Thessalonica ye sent once and again unto my necessity. Not because I desire a gift: but I desire fruit that may abound to your account. But I have all, and abound: I am full, having received of Epaphroditus the things which were sent from you, an odour of a sweet smell, a sacrifice acceptable, well pleasing to God. But my God shall supply all your need according to his riches in glory by Christ Jesus" Philippians 4:15-19.

As a missionary who travelled from place to place establishing and strengthening Churches, the Apostle Paul and his team had to either depend on what was given them from the collections at a place or sometimes engage in some form of work to earn money for their sustenance. Noteworthy was that the Philippians did not limit their giving to when the Apostle was present with them. They often sent resources to sustain the missionary work of Apostle Paul and the team. This would have been difficult to accomplish since there was no Global Banking System or Western Union Money Transfer kind of system to facilitate transfer of money. They would have to send someone bearing their collections to deliver the money to the Apostle Paul wherever he was.

The Apostle Paul referred to this unique relationship as a 'giving and receiving' relationship. Concerning their offerings He says – "an odor of a sweet smell, a sacrifice acceptable, well pleasing to God." In other words, it smells good to God any time you send an offering. When you sponsor the divine assignment of our mission, your offering smells like Noah's offering and makes the heart of God glad. As a result this should be your expectation – "My God shall supply all your need according to his riches in glory by Christ Jesus." Whenever God is glorified by our giving, He releases blessings. He supplies our needs. There is a miraculous provision to take care of our financial obligations.

Missionaries who take the gospel and supplies to the underprivileged in difficult regions of the world need partners to sponsor their missions. God works through those who live in prosperous parts of the world to sponsor these missionaries. It is important that we all who are blessed with the privilege of decent incomes and resources to regularly give to such missions so they can continue their assignment. This way God keeps our sources of income and revenue flowing regardless of the schemes of the enemy.

Manifestation Plan

Chapter
Two

MANIFESTATION ERA

" A nd it came to pass at the end of two full years, that Pharaoh dreamed: and, behold, he stood by the river. And, behold, there came up out of the river seven well favoured kine and fatfleshed; and they fed in a meadow. And, behold, seven other kine came up after them out of the river, ill favoured and leanfleshed; and stood by the other kine upon the brink of the river. And the ill favoured and leanfleshed kine did eat up the seven well favoured and fat kine. So Pharaoh awoke. And he slept and dreamed the second time: and, behold, seven ears of corn came up upon one stalk, rank and good. And, behold, seven thin ears and blasted with the east wind sprung up after them. And the seven thin ears devoured the seven rank and full ears. And Pharaoh awoke, and, behold, it was a dream. And it came to pass in the morning that his spirit was troubled; and he sent and called for all the magicians of Egypt, and all the wise men thereof: and Pharaoh told them his dream; but there was none that could interpret them unto Pharaoh. Then spake the chief butler unto Pharaoh, saying, I do remember my faults this day:

Pharaoh was wroth with his servants, and put me in ward in the captain of the guard's house, both me and the chief baker: And we dreamed a dream in one night, I and he; we dreamed each man according to the interpretation of his dream. And there was there with us a young man, an Hebrew, servant to the captain of the guard; and we told him, and he interpreted to us our dreams; to each man according to his dream he did interpret. And it came to pass, as he interpreted to us, so it was; me he restored unto mine office, and him he hanged. Then Pharaoh sent and called Joseph, and they brought him hastily out of the dungeon: and he shaved himself, and changed his raiment, and came in unto Pharaoh" Genesis 41:1-14.

The Pharaoh of Egypt has an unusual dream, which he knows is a divine encounter. Though he believes that it is a message of great significance, his magicians and advisors have no clue what the dream means. The message is somewhat coded. His spirit is troubled. His officials are aware of this predicament and are also troubled with him. Then the Chief Butler remembers the assignment of Joseph to mention him to the Pharaoh. This is the perfect timing for the assignment. The Chief Butler informs the Pharaoh of Joseph's capabilities. The Pharaoh sends for Joseph to be brought into his presence. This is Joseph's release order from prison. The pre-manifestation era of his life has come to an end. It is time for manifestation!

INTERPRETATION AND COUNSEL

The Pharaoh narrates his dream to Joseph and this is the interpretation Joseph reveals:

"And Joseph said unto Pharaoh, The dream of Pharaoh is one: God hath shewed Pharaoh what he is about to do. The seven good kine are seven years; and the seven good ears are seven years: the dream is one. And the seven thin and ill favoured kine that came up after them are seven years; and the seven empty ears blasted with the east wind shall be seven years of famine. This is the thing which I have spoken unto Pharaoh: What God is about to do he sheweth unto Pharaoh. Behold, there come seven years of great plenty throughout all the land of Egypt: And there shall arise after them seven years of famine; and all the plenty shall be forgotten in the land of Egypt; and the famine shall consume the land; And the plenty shall not be known in the land by reason of that famine following; for it shall be very grievous. And for that the dream was doubled unto Pharaoh twice; it is because the thing is established by God, and God will shortly bring it to pass" Genesis 41:25-32.

Seven fat cows and seven fat ears of corn mean that there will be seven years of abundance. The seven lean cows and the seven thin ears of corn mean that there will be seven years of famine following the seven years of abundance. Joseph remarks that the reason the message is double indicates that this dream is an established decision of God which would also come to pass shortly.

Joseph provides counsel to the Pharaoh as to how to administer the affairs of Egypt in the light of the dream. "Now therefore let Pharaoh look out a man discreet and wise, and set him over the land of Egypt. Let Pharaoh do this, and let him appoint officers over the land, and take up the fifth part of the land of Egypt in the seven plenteous years. And let them gather all the food of those good years that come, and lay up corn under the hand of Pharaoh, and let them keep food in the cities. And that food shall be for store to the land against the seven years of famine, which shall be in the land of Egypt; that the land perish not through the famine" Genesis 41:33-36.

Joseph suggests that the Pharaoh appoint a wise and discreet official over a government agency that would be responsible for procuring one-fifth of the produce of the land during the seven years of abundance. The food procured will be stored up against the seven years of famine. The Pharaoh is intrigued by this solution and he considers that Joseph's counsel is appropriate.

"And the thing was good in the eyes of Pharaoh, and in the eyes of all his servants. And Pharaoh said unto his servants, Can we find such a one as this is, a man in whom the Spirit of God is? And Pharaoh said unto Joseph, Forasmuch as God hath shewed thee all this, there is none so discreet and wise as thou art: Thou shalt be over my house, and according unto thy word shall all my people be ruled: only in the throne will I be greater than thou. And

Pharaoh said unto Joseph, See, I have set thee over all the land of Egypt. And Pharaoh took off his ring from his hand, and put it upon Joseph's hand, and arrayed him in vestures of fine linen, and put a gold chain about his neck; And he made him to ride in the second chariot which he had; and they cried before him, Bow the knee: and he made him ruler over all the land of Egypt. And Pharaoh said unto Joseph, I am Pharaoh, and without thee shall no man lift up his hand or foot in all the land of Egypt" Genesis 41:37-44.

This is the day Joseph has anticipated for all his life. The dream from God is manifesting just as God promised. Joseph is appointed as second in command over Egypt. The Pharaoh and his officials agree that Joseph is the only one with the ability to administer the revelation to save Egypt from the predicted drought. Joseph is given such awesome authority and responsibility. This is the place of fulfillment that God promises all those who accept their calling to fulfill divine destiny.

WISE AND DISCREET

The qualification Joseph recommends for whoever would administer Egypt to prevent a food crisis was that such a fellow should be distinguished as being wise and discreet. Let us firstly consider why Joseph requires that a man of wisdom should be placed in charge and then we would follow up to understand why such a fellow should be a person of discretion.

• Wisdom

In the dream of the Pharaoh we notice there are seven fat cows and seven fat ears of corn that signify a period of abundance. Seven is predominant in the dream and so it is important to consider what it means. The scriptures tell us that God created the earth within the framework of seven days. In the first six days, He is engaged in the literal work of creation but then in the seventh day He reserves it to Himself.

"Thus the heavens and the earth were finished, and all the host of them. And on the seventh day God ended his work which he had made; and he rested on the seventh day from all his work which he had made. And God blessed the seventh day, and sanctified it: because that in it he had rested from all his work which God created and made" Genesis 2:1-3.

For most people who work from Monday to Friday on a weekly basis, Friday is often the most loved day at work. This is because it is the last day of the traditional work week and people get to rest over the weekend. Similarly, God rested on the seventh day, He blessed it and sanctified it. He assigned the seventh day to Himself. He later commanded the Israelites to also observe the literal rest of the seventh day and fellowship with Him. That is the day in which He unveils His word and releases blessings. He sanctifies that day with His word, meaning that He cleans up that day. Everyone who comes to Him on that day would experience His sanctification or cleansing. This is awesome. The revelation of His word gives us an opportunity to repent from our sinful ways and make amends with God. Our path of life is directed by divine revelation to align with God's will. This is how we invoke the blessing of divine favor.

"Wisdom hath builded her house, she hath hewn out her seven pillars: She hath killed her beasts; she hath mingled her wine; she hath also furnished her table. She hath sent forth her maidens: she crieth upon the highest places of the city, Whoso is simple, let him turn in hither: as for him that wanteth understanding, she saith to him, Come, eat of my bread, and drink of the wine which I have mingled. Forsake the foolish, and live; and go in the way of understanding" Proverbs 9:1-6.

It is interesting to note that the house of wisdom is built upon seven pillars. Pillars are the foundations of a building. They constitute the superstructure that holds an edifice. Significantly if wisdom is built upon seven pillars, it indicates that wisdom is the house of God. This is where God dwells. Wisdom prepares food and reaches out to those who are interested to come and feast. Remember that God blessed the seventh day and sanctified it with His word. He also commanded the Israelites to always come in and feast with Him on the seventh day. It is obvious that the usage of seven in the dream of Pharaoh is reference to God inviting the Egyptians to feast with him for seven years. During the seven years of abundance, He would lavish wisdom upon the Egyptians in abundance and they would flourish in their endeavors.

This poses the question: what about the seven years of famine? Satan who is the enemy of God's goodness always cherishes to occupy God's place. That is why he rebelled against God. Satan has set up his kingdom to directly oppose God's kingdom. Satan constantly tries to mimic God's works and the results of such actions are directly opposite. That is the essence of the seven years of famine.

• Discretion

Let us consider the qualification of discretion. We have discovered that the usage of seven in the Pharaoh's dreams is reference to the wisdom of God. Wisdom is the superstructure of the house where God dwells. When you visit an edifice especially at the preliminary stages of construction, you will observe the foundations and pillars are cast with concrete and steel pillars. This phase of the construction process of any edifice is not pleasant to behold. The interesting phase of any edifice is while the beautifying fixtures are installed. You immediately see what impact they have on the building when installed. Within any building, there are several fixtures that allow us to utilize the building to the fullness of its potentials. These extra features incorporated into the design of a building that makes it useful to people is what is known as concepts of the design. The architect incorporates various concepts into the design of an edifice to make it useful to the extent that the owner requires.

When the superstructure of an edifice is constructed, an architect can switch the usage to suit different uses by altering the finishing. You will notice that commercial property developers would often put up the skeleton structure of an edifice and then advertise it as ready for various commercial uses. The tenant determines how the edifice will be configured to suit their use of the property. Assuming the property will be used as a medical office, manufacturing or retail business, an architect is engaged to design the empty space to suit that purpose. The architect who designs the space for a commercial purpose would have to exercise great discretion in his plan. Great discretion means that he would manage the space in such a way that it fulfills the purpose for which it is intended and have all the necessary conveniences. Low discretion means poor management of the space provided.

COWS AND CORN

In the Pharaoh's dream cows and corn are used as symbols to communicate God's intentions. Symbols are often employed in most divine revelations that we receive through dreams and visions. In the earliest forms of written communication, symbols of known objects were used to communicate among people. If I wanted to offer you ten cows in a deal, I would draw up ten cows on a canvas and send to you. This is how archaeologists read some ancient communication that is inscribed on walls and ancient materials.

Though the dream is given to Pharaoh, it is obvious that the intended recipient of the revelation is Joseph. The magicians and counselors of the Pharaoh have no clue as to the meaning of the dream. Joseph however does not struggle to understand this dream. He is conversant with the God who created heaven and the earth so He understands what seven means. He also understands what cows and corn signify. Cows were created on the sixth day of creation. This was the same day when man was also created. Joseph knew that cows signify the potential character traits of man. Through his training from his father Jacob, Joseph knew the significance of the cows in Pharaoh's dreams. God was about to flourish the corporate structures of human endeavors. He would lavish the wisdom by which human enterprises and organizations are established to flourish.

Corn is a part of vegetation on the third day of creation. On this day, God commanded the land to bring forth vegetation that bears fruit with seed. The three core components for fruitfulness are spelt out as being land, fruit and seed. In employing corn as an element of the message to the Pharaoh, God was articulating the intention to lavish Egypt with the concepts for fruitfulness in all endeavors.

A HEART OF DIVINE STRUCTURES AND CONCEPTS

The reason the magicians and advisors of Pharaoh could not interpret this dream was because it was outside their realm of comprehension. It is obvious that they could not fathom the relevance of the value seven, cows and corn. The Pharaoh quickly discerned that if Joseph understood the dream and provided counsel as to how to administer it, then Joseph qualified as possessing a heart of wisdom and discretion.

Joseph was taught by his father Jacob to abide in God's house that was built upon seven pillars. When Joseph served as a slave in Potiphar's house, the scriptures says that God was with him. Joseph knew how to invoke the presence of God and maintained fellowship with God. This is how he flourished while serving Potiphar. Joseph knew how to access the wisdom of God and apply to his responsibilities. His heart was structured in God.

Within every structure, there are various concepts for fruitfulness. One of the core qualifications for employing the services of a CEO is great discretion. Joseph knew how to apply divine concepts to his endeavors. Concepts are methods for doing things. Potiphar observed that Joseph was highly successful in his assignments. He knew what method to engage in the face of a challenge. His unusual discretionary ability was obvious.

THE SEVEN PILLARS

Within the tabernacle of Moses, the lamp-stand which was the only source of light in the Holy Place gives us insight into the Wisdom of God. When Jesus Christ visits John on the island of Patmos, He manifests in the midst of the lamp-stand of God's presence (Revelation 1). Isaiah the prophet speaks prophetically about how Jesus Christ would function and make decisions by employing the Seven Spirits of God.

"And there shall come forth a rod out of the stem of Jesse, and a Branch shall grow out of his roots: And the spirit of the LORD shall rest upon him, the spirit of wisdom and understanding, the spirit of counsel and might, the spirit of knowledge and of the fear of the LORD" Isaiah 11:1&2. The Seven Spirits of God are unveiled below in functional order:

1) Spirit of Knowledge
2) Spirit of Understanding
3) Spirit of Wisdom
4) Spirit of the Lord
5) Spirit of the Fear of the Lord
6) Spirit of Counsel
7) Spirit of Might

- **The Spirit of Knowledge:**

When God speaks to us on a particular issue for the first time, it is the manifestation of the Spirit of Knowledge. Usually such a revelation might be a scriptural verse or with the use of symbols.

- **The Spirit of Understanding:**

Assuming we do not grasp the meaning of the revelation from God, we have to seek the Spirit of Understanding. Most often, a simple prayer to God after receiving a complex scripture or complicated dream will unveil the Spirit of Understanding. The Spirit of Understanding brings more clarity to a scripture, vision or dream revelation.

- **The Spirit of Wisdom:**

Now that we have gained understanding, we are ready to apply the revelation to our life. The Spirit of Wisdom helps us micromanage the revelation. He guides us through little nudges as to the appropriate steps to take at the right time.

- **The Spirit of the Lord:**

Most often when we start to take steps that align with the leading of the Holy Spirit, the enemy who keeps us in captivity would notice that we are breaking out of the cycle of circumstances he has chained us with. The enemy orchestrates all kinds of external challenges that are intended to discourage our pursuits in alignment with the Holy Spirit. To overcome the enemy, we invoke the Spirit of the Lord by testifying of what He has done in the past. "And they overcame him by the blood of the Lamb, and by the word of their testimony..." Revelation 12:11. Our confession of God's testimonies in the scriptures as well as in our personal lives is how we defeat the schemes of opposition.

- **The Spirit of the Fear of The Lord (Reverence):**

The word fear is not used in the sense of a phobia or scare or inhibition. Rather, it is the sense of reverence for God. The Spirit of the Fear of the Lord is also known as the Spirit of Reverence. Usually when the enemy is unable to discourage us by orchestrating external challenges against us, assuming our faith confessions of God's testimonies are positive, then he resorts to mind games. He engages us in a psychological warfare. Such questions begin to spring up in our minds – Why is God not coming through for me? Has God abandoned me? Does God not recognize all that I am doing in fulfilling His assignments? Does God really love me? Has God not abandoned me? These questions are intended to dismantle our confidence in God and ultimately weaken our hands and feet that are in pursuit of divine purpose. The Spirit of Reverence is the tenacity to keep on fulfilling every divine assignment as though we are not experiencing challenges.

"Cast not away therefore your confidence, which hath great recompense of reward. For ye have need of patience, that, after ye have done the will of God, ye might receive the promise. For yet a little while, and he that shall come will come, and will not tarry. Now the just shall live by faith: but if any man draw back, my soul shall have no pleasure in him. But we are not of them who draw back unto perdition; but of them that believe to the saving of the soul" Hebrew 10:35-39.

Simply put, we must ignore the devil and his schemes against us. Maintain a great attitude and entrench ourselves in deep confidence in God by continuing to pursue all that God has called us to fulfill.

- **The Spirit of Counsel:**

When you overcome the psychological warfare from the enemy through 'staying power', you are ready for the Spirit of Counsel. The Spirit of Counsel is a function of the Holy Spirit that guides us to specific people with whom God has endowed with the potential to help us overcome our challenges. Such people or organizations would gladly work with us to engage the situation. Do not underestimate whoever God recommends as a potential source of help to overcome your situation. Also, it is important that you work with the counsel of such people.

- ## The Spirit of Might:

Once you are in collaboration with those who were suggested to you by the Spirit of Counsel, you are ready for the Spirit of Might. 'Might' means 'power in action.' When you work together with your divinely assigned helpers, God's power would be unleashed to defeat every plot devised by the enemy to stop your advancement. You will be victorious against any opposition by the Spirit of Might.

SOLVING PROBLEMS, THE RIGHT WAY

As we have read previously, Isaiah prophesied about how Jesus Christ would not resolve the issues of life by a carnal approach, but would always engage the Seven Spirits of God. Let us look at this scenario where Jesus is confronted with a massive challenge: "And Jesus, when he came out, saw much people, and was moved with compassion toward them, because they were as sheep not having a shepherd: and he began to teach them many things. And when the day was now far spent, his disciples came unto him, and said, This is a desert place, and now the time is far passed: Send them away, that they may go into the country round about, and into the villages, and buy themselves bread: for they have nothing to eat. He answered and said unto them, Give ye them to eat. And they say unto him, Shall we go and buy two hundred pennyworth of bread, and give them to eat? He saith unto them, How many loaves have ye? go and see. And when they knew, they say, Five, and two fishes. And he commanded them to make all sit down by companies upon the green grass. And they sat down in ranks, by hundreds, and by fifties. And when he had taken the five loaves and the two fishes, he looked up to heaven, and blessed, and brake the loaves, and gave them to his disciples to set before them; and the two fishes divided he among them all. And they did all eat, and were filled. And they took up twelve baskets full of the fragments, and of the fishes. And they that did eat of the loaves were about five thousand men" Mark 6:34-44.

Jesus had just finished ministering to a massive crowd that had gathered to hear Him. Night was drawing closer, so the disciples suggested that the crowd be dispersed to go back to their homes. Jesus had another thought: "Give ye them to eat." The disciples objected: "Shall we go and buy two hundred pennyworth of bread, and give them to eat?" In other words, with all the money that we have in our ministry coffers, it would be impossible to feed this crowd of over four thousand people. Jesus asks them to find out how much food was available. They come back with interesting numbers: five loaves and two fishes! Jesus is not perturbed by the quantity of food resources available. "And he commanded them to make all sit down by companies upon the green grass. And they sat down in ranks, by hundreds, and by fifties."

At this point, everyone in the crowd was thinking what to do next. People were moving up and down and so they were disorganized. Jesus knew the consequence of dispersing this crowd away from this desert location. Some may faint on the way out of hunger. Such an occurrence would cast a negative shadow on the crusades of Jesus and give the authorities and religious leaders a reason to attack Jesus.

The first step to take when confronted with challenges is to organize the problems, and that is how Jesus approached the challenge. He commanded His disciples to organize the crowd in such a way that aligns with God's order. On their journey from Egypt to the Promised Land, God taught the Israelites how to position themselves around His tabernacle so that He could show Himself strong in their midst. God's angels are supernatural entities who function within the framework of divine order. Wherever there is disorder, demons flourish. Every challenge or problem is a consequence of some sort of disorder.

The command was to have the people sit down companies. This is the overall objective. However, this command was implemented to reflect divine order - "And they sat in ranks, by hundreds, and by fifties." Though this order may look like a literal numerical arrangement, it was an arrangement based on their three-fold existence as humans. We are three-dimensional human beings – We are Spirit, we have a Soul and we live in a Body. "But ye are a chosen generation, a royal priesthood, an holy nation, a peculiar people; that ye should shew forth the praises of him who hath called you out of darkness into his marvelous light" 1 Peter 2:9. With our Spirit we have a relationship with God and serve as priests in His house. With our Soul we have a relationship with our fellow man. With our Body we have a relationship with the earth and material things.

- **'Ranks'**

This was significant of their priestly disposition. In the Old Testament, the Levites were assigned the spiritual function of serving God on behalf of the Israelites. In the New Testament Dispensation, the believer has direct access to God by his spirit through Jesus Christ our High Priest. Jesus Christ has endowed every believer with spiritual gifts by which we can serve God as priests. "But unto every one of us is given grace according to the measure of the gift of Christ. Wherefore he saith, When he ascended up on high, he led captivity captive, and gave gifts unto men" Ephesians 4:7&8. We are able to serve God and glorify Him with these spiritual gifts. Every believer has a priestly disposition based on the spiritual gifts they have received from Jesus Christ. As Christians, we belong to local Churches where we are expected to serve in a function based on our spiritual gifts. This is how we serve God as priests.

- **'Hundreds'**

This was significant of their prophetic capacity. We all live in the framework of family relationships and a society of friends and neighbors. This is our world of people that constitute our community. We are expected to reach out to those in our world with the gospel and the love of our Lord Jesus Christ. Every believer has a message from the scriptures for those who live in our world. There is a "Thus says the Lord" potential in every believer for our neighbors. Our relationship with the community is what is known as prophetic capacity. The story about Cornelius in Acts 10 is relevant to this truth:

"There was a certain man in Caesarea called Cornelius, a centurion of the band called the Italian band, A devout man, and one that feared God with all his house, which gave much alms to the people, and prayed to God always. He saw in a vision evidently about the ninth hour of the day an angel of God coming in to him, and saying unto him, Cornelius. And when he looked on him, he was afraid, and said, What is it, Lord? And he said unto him, Thy prayers and thine alms are come up for a memorial before God. And now send men to Joppa, and call for one Simon, whose surname is Peter: He lodgeth with one Simon a tanner, whose house is by the sea side: he shall tell thee what thou oughtest to do. And when the angel which spake unto Cornelius was departed, he called two of his household servants, and a devout soldier of them that waited on him continually; And when he had declared all these things unto them, he sent them to Joppa. On the morrow, as they went on their journey, and drew nigh unto the city, Peter went up upon the housetop to pray about the sixth hour: And he became very hungry, and would have eaten: but while they made ready, he fell into a trance, And saw heaven opened, and a certain vessel descending upon him, as it had been a great sheet knit at the four corners, and let down to the earth: Wherein were all manner of fourfooted beasts of the earth, and wild beasts, and creeping things, and fowls of the air. And there came a voice to him, Rise, Peter; kill, and eat. But Peter said, Not so, Lord; for I have never eaten any thing that is common or unclean. And the voice spake unto him again the second time, What God hath cleansed, that call not thou common. This was done thrice: and the vessel was received up again into heaven. Now while Peter doubted in himself what this vision which he had seen should mean, behold, the men which were sent from Cornelius had made enquiry for Simon's house, and stood before the gate, And called, and asked whether Simon, which was surnamed Peter, were lodged there. While Peter thought on the vision, the Spirit said unto him, Behold, three men seek thee. Arise therefore, and get thee down, and go with them, doubting nothing: for I have sent them. Then Peter went down to the men which were sent unto him from Cornelius; and said, Behold, I am he whom ye seek: what is the cause wherefore ye are come? And they said, Cornelius the centurion, a just man, and one that feareth God, and of good report among all the nation of the Jews, was warned from God by an holy angel to send for thee into his house, and to hear words of thee. Then called he them in, and lodged them. And on the morrow Peter went away with them, and certain brethren from Joppa accompanied him. And the morrow after they entered into Caesarea. And Cornelius waited for them, and he had called together his kinsmen and near friends. And as Peter was coming in, Cornelius met him, and fell down at his feet, and worshipped him. But Peter took him up, saying, Stand up; I myself also am a man. And as he talked with him, he went in, and found many that were come together" Acts 10:1-27.

Cornelius is described as a centurion. A Centurion was a soldier assigned to one hundred other soldiers. The number of soldiers that are placed under an officer's command reflects their leadership capacity. Cornelius was a leader who demonstrated his leadership capacity not only with his soldiers but also in his community. God took notice of this and selected him as the first Gentile family to receive salvation. Notice what the angel said about him: "Thy prayers and thine alms are come up for a memorial before God." Though he was not a Jew, Cornelius was a prayerful man and generous in alms giving. Prayer is communication with God. The more we engage God in the dialogue of prayer, we open ourselves to hear from Him. Though God often speaks to us traditionally through dreams, visions, prophetic words, He also speaks to us by influencing our thoughts. Cornelius had a reputation of a generous alms-giver. This meant that he availed himself as a conduit for the flow of resources to meet the needs of the needy in his community. Cornelius demonstrated his love for God and man so God chose his family as the door-way for the gospel to reach the Gentile world. Notice how he gathers so much people to receive the ministry of the Apostle Peter.

Every believer has the potential of 'hundreds' as their prophetic capacity. It is how we are all placed to minister the love of Christ to the world around us through the gospel and good deeds. While some of us are reaching out with this love to the fullest of our capacity, others are struggling to dispense the love of Christ to their constituency. Whenever we meet those who have urgent survival needs, it is known as 'prophetic opportunity.' Our positive response to help such people becomes a demonstration of our 'prophetic capacity.' Ultimately, the level of your influence in society is evidence of how much you have availed yourself to become a blessing to people.

- **'Fifties'**

This was significant of their destiny and kingly heritage. The number fifty is used in reference to the Jubilee. The Jubilee was celebrated every fifty years in Israel. It mandated land restoration for those who had leased their inheritance or lost their inheritance during hard times. When the Israelites came to the Promised Land, the land was shared among the tribes such that each family had their own allotment. The natural potentials of the land allotted to each tribe determined their vocation. For instance, a tribe like Zebulun which inherited coastal lands became a sea faring people. 'Fifties' was reference to the destiny of each tribe so when the people were organized in fifties, it was according to their economic segments.

DIVINE SEQUENCE FOR ORGANIZING PROBLEMS

To understand how Jesus and the disciples organized the crowd in divine order, let us consider the way in which God led them from Egypt through the wilderness to conquer the Promised Land.

"And the LORD spake unto Moses and unto Aaron, saying, Every man of the children of Israel shall pitch by his own standard, with the ensign of their father's house: far off about the tabernacle of the congregation shall they pitch. And on the east side toward the rising of the sun shall they of the standard of the camp of Judah pitch throughout their armies: and Nahshon the son of Amminadab shall be captain of the children of Judah" Numbers 2:1-3.

All the tribes were designated camping positions as a coordinate of the tabernacle, which was pitched at the center of the camp. Furthermore, God instructed Moses to make silver trumpets by which specific sounds would be made for divine alignments. "And the LORD spake unto Moses, saying, Make thee two trumpets of silver; of a whole piece shalt thou make them: that thou mayest use them for the calling of the assembly, and for the journeying of the camps. And when they shall blow with them, all the assembly shall assemble themselves to thee at the door of the tabernacle of the congregation. And if they blow but with one trumpet, then the princes, which are heads of the thousands of Israel, shall gather themselves unto thee. When ye blow an alarm, then the camps that lie on the east parts shall go forward. When ye blow an alarm the second time, then the camps that lie on the south side shall take their journey: they shall blow an alarm for their journeys. But when the congregation is to be gathered together, ye shall blow, but ye shall not sound an alarm. And the sons of Aaron, the priests, shall blow with the trumpets; and they shall be to you for an ordinance for ever throughout your generations. And if ye go to war in your land against the enemy that oppresseth you, then ye shall blow an alarm with the trumpets; and ye shall be remembered before the LORD your God, and ye shall be saved from your enemies. Also in the day of your gladness, and in your solemn days, and in the beginnings of your months, ye shall blow with the trumpets over your burnt offerings, and over the sacrifices of your peace offerings; that they may be to you for a memorial before your God: I am the LORD your God" Numbers 10:1-10.

The trumpet was the official instrument for making sounds by which Israel was organized for general instruction, leadership instruction, alpha movement, omega movement, warfare and prosperity. Since their tents were pitched around the tabernacle by tribal arrangement, they would hear the sounds made by the trumpets and order themselves accordingly.

RESOLVING PROBLEMS BY FIFTY

Let us think of this configuration in a practical sense. With the tribes arranged around the tabernacle, they form a wall around the house of God. As part of the conquest of the Promised Land, King David conquered Jerusalem and designated it capital of Israel. Jerusalem was designed according to this pattern where the temple was in the middle and surrounded by the city wall with twelve gates. These gates were significant of the twelve tribes. Assuming the enemy was to attack, it would be from outside the camp and target specific gates or all of them. Most often the enemy comes against us with external challenges that are pitched against our gates.

When under an attack the first step is to make an assessment of the attack. You want to evaluate the strength of the enemy that has come up against your gates. "A wise man scaleth the city of the mighty, and casteth down the strength of the confidence thereof" Proverbs 21:22. This is the fundamental step in warfare. Jesus also taught the essence of this fundamental principle for warfare. "Or what king, going to make war against another king, sitteth not down first, and consulteth whether he be able with ten thousand to meet him that cometh against him with twenty thousand Or else, while the other is yet a great way off, he sendeth an ambassage, and desireth conditions of peace" Luke 14:31&32.

If Jerusalem was under attack, the king would want to determine against which gate the enemy had pitched. The king would require those at this gate to evaluate the potential strength of the enemy. Information such as their number, type of weapons and their formation would help the king to determine how to either defend that gate or counter-attack the enemy. You can only defeat an enemy after properly weighing his capabilities. If you can figure out the devices of the enemy then you can harness the appropriate resources to overcome him.

The proper approach to problems is not to start crying out to God. The scriptural wisdom is to evaluate the enemy that has come against you. Like a king whose city is under attack, you want to find out which gate is under attack. Then you want to assess the strength of this enemy. Furthermore, you want to consult with the custodians of this gate as to the state of the gate in relation with the strength of the enemy. 'Can the enemy overcome this gate with his strength?' Are we well-fortified at this gate to wade off this attack? What can we do to reinforce this gate to resist the attack? Assuming the king feels confident with the answers he receives after having dialogue with his counselors at this gate, he proceeds to engage the enemy with his resources at that gate.

In the first chapter of this book, we learnt about the Pre-manifestation era of our lives where we must do the diligence of profiling those who God has placed in our world to determine their potentials. All such people who God has blessed us with are a part of our government. These people are the gates of our lives and destiny assignment. When the enemy comes up against us with challenges, the first line of action is to consult with those whose divine potentials place them at the gate under attack. Assuming we can get help from our counselors to wade off the enemy, then the problem is solved. This is how we solve by fifty.

RESOLVING PROBLEMS BY 'RANKS'

However, if after consulting with our counselors or government, we realize that the enemy has greater potential to overcome us, then we must take the second step to solve by 'ranks.' We approach the priest with our condition of overwhelming challenges. Any problem that we cannot overcome by our government is a spiritual problem. The tabernacle is designed with seven major protocols for fellowship with God.

1) The Brazen Laver
2) The Altar of Sacrifice
3) The Lampstand
4) The Table of Showbread

5) The Altar of Incense
6) The Veil
7) The Ark of the Covenant.

• The Brazen Laver

This is the first object of fellowship in the tabernacle. It is the place for meditation and reflections of our life based on the word of God. This is where we find the ministry of the Teacher and all those whose spiritual gifts incline them to teach God's word. It is at this point in the tabernacle that we develop our spiritual skill and how to function in the spirit of excellence.

• The Altar of Sacrifice

This is the second object of our spiritual fellowship. This is where animal sacrifices where offered upon the altar and their blood for the remission of sins. The altar of sacrifice was significant of the cross where Jesus died and paid the price for our sins. Typically, this is where the Evangelist functions. Those with evangelistic gifts often have an unusual burden for the salvation of souls. Forgiveness, healing and deliverance takes place at this altar.

• The Lampstand

This is the third object of fellowship in the tabernacle. It was a seven-branched candlestick that provided light in the Holy Place of the tabernacle. This is the place where issues of spiritual, emotional, financial and physical barrenness are resolved. This is the place for prophetic revelation and so those with prophetic gifts and psalmists function in this part of the tabernacle. Our visionary capabilities are enhanced here as well as the ability to glorify God by divine inspiration.

- **The Table of Showbread**

This is the fourth object of fellowship in the tabernacle. The bread here is our spiritual providence. Divine wisdom to flourish at the space that God has assigned as our territory to reign as kings. This is where we receive inspiring instruction from God's word. As believers, we gather for fellowship at least once a week to receive such a message from God. The Pastor and those gifted as such usually act as the head of the local Church and are responsible for feeding and leading the flock so the table of shewbread is that place in the tabernacle.

- **The Altar of Incense**

This is the fifth object of worship in the tabernacle. This is where we come into full alignment with divine order. We glorify God with inspired righteousness, inspired intercession, inspired adoration and inspired offerings. This is how we incline ourselves to align with divine order, foster spiritual revivals and destroy the influence of apostasy, divination and occult in our space. Those with Apostolic gifts usually function here.

• The Veil

This is the sixth object of fellowship in the tabernacle. This is where we engage every inhibition of the mind. Here we overcome human oppression, domineering, controlling and manipulating spirits. Usually, gifted Administrators function here. Joseph is an example of a gifted Administrator who appropriated God's word to bear on the government and the economic conditions of Egypt.

• The Ark of the Covenant

This is the seventh object of fellowship. This is where judgment took place. It was a place where God's mercy was invoked to bear upon our lives and conditions. We experience divine rest, release from spiritual debt, restoration from all sorts of disenfranchisement and issues of disinheritance. Those with gifts of mercy and helps function from here.

These seven objects of fellowship are the seven places where all challenges of life are resolved supernaturally. Whenever we bring our problems before the priest, he would discern them as to where they are resolved in the tabernacle and assign us to the priest who is particularly gifted help us.

When a challenge is deemed as spiritual, it is an indication of where we fall short of God's glory. If we fall short of God's glory at the Brazen Laver, then we must be assigned to a Teacher to help us fortify our intuition. If we fall short at the Altar of Sacrifice, then we would be assigned to the Evangelist to fix our discernment. If we fall short at the lampstand, we are assigned a Prophet to help us with vision. If we fall short at the Table of Shewbread, the Pastor helps us fix our spiritual authority. If we fall short at the Altar of Incense, the Apostle helps us with divine alignment. If we fall short at the Veil, the gifted Administrator helps us with restoration of our Dominion. If we fall short at the Ark of the Covenant, the gifted helpers provide resources.

Whenever our challenges are resolves spiritually, the enemy loses the legitimacy to remain at our gates. He immediately knows it is time to dismantle his framework of attack. In the days of Gideon when the Midianites besieged Israel, the angel who visited Gideon gave instruction to dismantle the Baal worship of his father's house and offer a sacrifice to God. When Gideon obeyed this instruction, the foothold of Baal was uprooted from the land and it was easy to overcome the Midianites with only three hundred men. (Judges 6&7)

RESOLVING PROBLEMS BY 'HUNDREDS'

Whenever we take the appropriate spiritual steps to resolve our spiritual deficiencies, the enemy's legitimate grounds for attacking us comes to an end. The enemy's mandate expires. At this point the enemy becomes vulnerable and makes mistakes which become our advantage. King David experienced such a scenario when his stronghold was attacked by the Amalekites who stole his possessions and burned Ziklag with fire. It was a distressing moment for both David and his soldiers because they had lost everything as well as their family members to the enemy. David sought God through the ephod and God instructed him to pursue the enemy.

"But David pursued, he and four hundred men: for two hundred abode behind, which were so faint that they could not go over the brook Besor. And they found an Egyptian in the field, and brought him to David, and gave him bread, and he did eat; and they made him drink water; And they gave him a piece of a cake of figs, and two clusters of raisins: and when he had eaten, his spirit came again to him: for he had eaten no bread, nor drunk any water, three days and three nights. And David said unto him, To whom belongest thou? and whence art thou? And he said, I am a young man of Egypt, servant to an Amalekite; and my master left me, because three days agone I fell sick. We made an invasion upon the south of the Cherethites, and upon the coast which belongeth to Judah, and upon the south of Caleb; and we burned Ziklag with fire. And David said to him, Canst thou bring me down to this company? And he said, Swear unto me by God, that thou wilt neither kill me, nor deliver me into the hands of my master, and I will bring thee down to this company. And when he had brought him down, behold, they were spread abroad upon all the earth, eating and drinking, and dancing, because of all the great spoil that they had taken out of the land of the Philistines, and out of the land of Judah. And David smote them from the twilight even unto the evening of the next day: and there escaped not a man of them, save four hundred young men, which rode upon camels, and fled. And David recovered all that the Amalekites had carried away: and David rescued his two wives. And there was nothing lacking to them, neither small nor great, neither sons nor daughters, neither spoil, nor any thing that they had taken to them: David recovered all" 1 Samuel 30:10-19.

By divine inspiration, David and his men set off in pursuit of the Amalekites who had robbed them. They found an Egyptian in the field who was sick and had been abandoned by his master who was part of the Amalekites that had robbed David. This was a prophetic opportunity for David. David and his men took care of this Egyptian and revived him with food and drink. As soldiers who had lost their wives, children and material possessions, the condition of this Egyptian should not have been their concern. However, David had learnt the essence of deploying 'prophetic capacity' whenever there was a 'prophetic opportunity.' This is the reason he stopped their pursuit of the Amalekites and took care of this sick

Egyptian. The Amalekites in their wickedness abandoned the sick Egyptian and left him to die in the field. Eventually this Egyptian brought David and his men to the location of the Amalekites and David recovered all that was lost. This is how the enemy makes mistakes that become our opportunity for recovery.

Summarily, the way to solve problems is by leveraging our kingly heritage 'fifty' as the first step, the second step is by our priestly ranks and the third step is by prophetic capacity 'hundreds'. We tackle our problems from outside our gates, then in the tabernacle and finally by taking advantage of prophetic opportunities that come our way.

THE ATTITUDE OF SCALING CHALLENGES

Whenever we are confronted with huge challenges, the attitude of our heart determines if we overcome them or not. During their journey from Egypt through the wilderness, the Lord taught the Israelites about the disposition of their heart in the light of His promises.

"If thou shalt say in thine heart, These nations are more than I; how can I dispossess them? Thou shalt not be afraid of them: but shalt well remember what the LORD thy God did unto Pharaoh, and unto all Egypt; The great temptations which thine eyes saw, and the signs, and the wonders, and the mighty hand, and the stretched out arm, whereby the LORD thy God brought thee out: so shall the LORD thy God do unto all the people of whom thou art afraid. Moreover the LORD thy God will send the hornet among them, until they that are left, and hide themselves from thee, be destroyed. Thou shalt not be affrighted at them: for the LORD thy God is among you, a mighty God and terrible. And the LORD thy God will put out those nations before thee by little and little: thou mayest not consume them at once, lest the beasts of the field increase upon thee. But the LORD thy God shall deliver them unto thee, and shall destroy them with a mighty destruction, until they be destroyed" Deuteronomy 7:17-23.

First of all, fear is an attitude of defeat. Fear strips us of our connection to the divine attributes by which God works through us to orchestrate victory over our enemies. God told the Israelites to never entertain fear in their hearts concerning the inhabitants of the Promised Land. We must never magnify any challenge above God who has promised to give us victory in all situations. God told the Israelites that no matter how huge the challenge, they should always remember His great acts and testimonies of the past to galvanize their faith.

Secondly, disorderliness is the play-ground of the enemy. Whenever we are disorganized, the enemy flourishes in our midst and manifests as challenges. Divine alignment is the key to divine intervention. The trumpet was the instrument that made the sounds of order. God established the sounds of order with the Israelites to bring them into divine alignment.

God's angels are very powerful beings that execute God's intentions for us always. However, they are orderly beings who function where they identify divine order. God's angels are already assigned to us as believers who have been baptized into Christ. When we are not organized according to a divine formation, angels cannot operate in our midst.

Several years ago, I attended a convention of independent Churches which took place at a high school boarding facility. I arrived early at the guest house and the host requested that I accompany him to the convention grounds. When we entered the main auditorium, I heard the Holy Spirit whisper to my heart saying: "I am not here." Wow, that hit me like a ton of bricks. I was scheduled to speak that night, which was the opening session. Without the Holy Spirits Presence, it would be a disaster! I quickly asked Him, what is wrong? He said: "look at the chairs." The room had been cleaned, set up for the service but the seating rows and columns were crooked. I got some help and we started aligning the columns and rows of chairs. Strangely, whenever we completed any section, I will notice the presence of the Holy Spirit saturated the space. That evening when I ministered, the presence, power and glory of God was so intense. The following day when we were having breakfast, I noticed a cold attitude from the other Ministers who were present. I had the feeling that something was wrong so I asked them. After some silence, one of the Ministers spoke out and asked me: "Why did you do that yesterday?" I said, "What did I do?" He went on to say – "Yesterday, you preached my message." Then a second Minister joined and said, "Yes and mine too. You set such a high standard yesterday at the meeting and now I do not know what to do. I have nothing to preach." Now I knew what their issue was. It was not because I had preached their message, rather, it was the intensity of God's presence, power and glory that had manifested. The obedience of aligning the hall to conform to divine order enabled the angels to flourish in the atmosphere of the meeting to the amazement of these Ministers.

God told the Israelites that He would sent the hornet among their enemies to defeat them. The hornet was the sound of God's trumpet that judges those who are in disorder. Assuming the Israelites conducted themselves in divine alignment to the sounds of the trumpet, then the same sound will be to their enemies as a sound of judgment. Those who align themselves with the sounds of divine order automatically constitute the armies of the Lord of Hosts. "Blessed is the people that know the joyful sound: they shall walk, O LORD, in the light of thy countenance" Psalm 89:15. The Captain of the Host leads them to overcome their enemies. In the story of how Israel overcame the city of Jericho, you may have wondered the answer of the Captain of the Host, when Joshua encountered Him. "And it came to pass, when Joshua was by Jericho, that he lifted up his eyes and looked, and, behold, there stood a man over against him with his sword drawn in his hand: and Joshua went unto him, and said unto him, Art thou for us, or for our adversaries? And he said, Nay; but as captain of the host of the LORD am I now come. And Joshua fell on his face to the earth, and did worship, and said unto him, What saith my Lord unto his servant?" Joshua 5:13&14.

The wisdom here is that, the Captain of the Host leads those who conduct themselves in alignment with divine order to victory against their enemies. God's angels take sides and fight alongside those who are in alignment.

Thirdly, we learn from Moses: "And the LORD thy God will put out those nations before thee by little and little: thou mayest not consume them at once, lest the beasts of the field increase upon thee." No matter how huge a challenge is, God helps to tackle them little by little. This was the same attitude of Jesus when confronted with a massive crowd that had to be fed with five loaves and two fishes – "And he commanded them to make all sit down by companies upon the green grass." In other words, break up the crowd into groups. If the people are not segmented, the picture is that of a chaotic overwhelming challenge. Think of what happened after the people are organized, they are now seated on the grass, relaxed and so they can brainstorm about the group's condition. Remember that they are organized based on 'fifties', 'ranks' and 'hundreds.'

The challenges are being tackled three-dimensionally that is; professionally, spiritually and prophetically and so it leaves little room for the enemy to survive. When a challenge is tackled in these three ways, we scale the enemy and reduce him to segments, which we can handle within our abilities. God entrenches the angels into each segment and victory becomes inevitable.

SEVEN YEARS OF ABUNDANCE

"Let Pharaoh do this, and let him appoint officers over the land, and take up the fifth part of the land of Egypt in the seven plenteous years. And let them gather all the food of those good years that come, and lay up corn under the hand of Pharaoh, and let them keep food in the cities. And that food shall be for store to the land against the seven years of famine, which shall be in the land of Egypt; that the land perish not through the famine" Genesis 41:34-36

Joseph counseled the Pharaoh to invest in twenty percent of all the abundance of the first seven years. This is not the conventional wisdom of governance with the Egyptians. The conventional wisdom is that Pharaoh collects taxes from the people and builds up the treasures of Egypt. Joseph recommended the opposite that is, to invest in the corn produced by the Egyptians. This is how Egypt would be preserved through the years of drought. The story of Elisha and the indebted widow sheds light on this wisdom:

"Now there cried a certain woman of the wives of the sons of the prophets unto Elisha, saying, Thy servant my husband is dead; and thou knowest that thy servant did fear the LORD: and the creditor is come to take unto him my two sons to be bondmen. And Elisha said unto her, What shall I do for thee? tell me, what hast thou in the house? And she said, Thine handmaid hath not any thing in the house, save a pot of oil. Then he said, Go, borrow thee vessels abroad of all thy neighbours, even empty vessels; borrow not a few. And when thou art come in, thou shalt shut the door upon thee and upon thy sons, and shalt pour out into all those vessels, and thou shalt set aside that which is full. So she went from him, and shut the door upon her and upon her sons, who brought the vessels to her; and she poured out. And it came to pass, when the vessels were full, that she said unto her son, Bring me yet a vessel. And he said unto her, There is not a vessel more. And the oil stayed. Then she came and told the man of God. And he said, Go, sell the oil, and pay thy debt, and live thou and thy children of the rest" 2 Kings 4:1-7.

The widow in this story was in debt and the creditors had come to take her two sons into bond service. It was the practice of that era that when you could not pay your debt, you were made a bond servant to work and clear up the debt. This widow came to Elisha because she was seeking divine intervention. Elisha asked her to take stock of her resources "what hast thou in the house?" She answered: "Thine handmaid hath not anything in the house, save a pot of oil." She had no material substance of value to the creditors. The only asset was a pot of oil, which is significant of the anointing of God. This anointing is always present once there is evidence of life. "But ye have an unction from the Holy One, and ye know all things. But the anointing which ye have received of him abideth in you, and ye need not that any man teach you: but as the same anointing teacheth you of all things, and is truth, and is no lie, and even as it hath taught you, ye shall abide in him" 1 John 2:20&27.

A core function of the anointing is to teach us. Elisha tells her what to do with her anointing: "Go, borrow thee vessels abroad of all thy neighbors, even empty vessels; borrow not a few. And when thou art come in, thou shalt shut the door upon thee and upon thy sons, and shalt pour out into all those vessels, and thou shalt set aside that which is full." This widow's neighbors had empty vessels waiting for her to fill. She had not yet impacted them with her anointing and this is the reason she was in debt. Elisha counsels her to go and seek opportunity to impact her neighbors. She should "borrow not a few." That meant she should seek to invest in as many neighbors as she possibly could. As in the case of Joseph investing in the Egyptians, this widow was counseled to invest in her neighbors. Our neighbors are our government. They are our natural support system. Neighbors will usually come to our aid, when we cry out in the face of trouble.

To overcome her indebtedness, Elisha counsels this widow to make a huge investment into her neighbors. All her neighbors had an empty jar waiting to be filled up with her oil. God has designed our lives such that we are all interdependent. Most often we find ourselves engaged in work just to survive. Our mindset is to be responsible only by mainstream standards such as pay our bills and build a financial nest. Some people get fortunate and achieve these goals but then others find it elusive and often get derailed by unexpected circumstances and become trapped in debt. The biggest problem in our society today is DEBT! Debt is the state where you are spending more than you earn. There are many institutions and programs that are designed to help people overcome their indebtedness and may bring temporary relief to those saddled with institutional debt. However, it is impossible to permanently overcome the debt to your society by a typical financial debt consolidation program.

Our real debt is the failure to invest our anointing into our neighbors. Investing our God-given potentials into our world is the fundamental way we overcome debt. Just as Elisha counsels the widow to invest in her neighbors, Joseph counseled the Pharaoh to invest in the Egyptians. The oil of the widow kept flowing into as many vessels as she had gathered from her neighbors. As soon as the last vessel was filled, the oil stopped flowing. This means that the oil would have kept flowing, as long as there were vessels to be filled. We see here the relationship of our vision with our scope of impact. God has blessed everyone with unlimited potentials but then, the extent to which we would impact our generation is based on our individual vision and scope.

HE BLESSED, BRAKE AND GAVE

Investing in those who belong to our world starts from within. In the story where Jesus orchestrated the multiplication of five loaves and two fishes to feed thousands of people, there is a pattern consistent with how He administers resources - He blessed, brake and gave.

- **He Blessed**

Jesus always blessed resources as a first step. Blessing involves words and actions. To bless a resource involves verbal acknowledgement of the source that is God, and the action is to assign His covenant portions. We owe our life, material resources and time to God who is our source. It is our core responsibility to bless God with all that He furnishes us.

- **He Brake**

Jesus brake the loaves according to the number of His disciples. The disciples were His government. The second function of the anointing, leads us to impact our government of neighbors. Our government of neighbors constitute those people who are closely related to us and gravitate towards us naturally. We learnt earlier on about 'fifty', which are those people who connect with us by destiny or royal heritage. In any typical government we would have functions such as administration, transportation, housing, commerce, health and education.

In the same way, as individuals we are surrounded with people who are professionals in these same areas. All our basic needs also factor into these areas. Essentially, these people are our natural government. If we ignore them from their potential standpoint and only relate to them socially, it would be to our own detriment.

In the first chapter we looked at the various ways the enemy launches his schemes against us – Assignment, People, Culture, Work, Reputation and Money. Our neighbors are our natural line of defense against the enemy. In our manifestation plan, we have to place our government of neighbors in their appropriate gates based on their potentials. We invest resources into their lives based on the leading of the anointing. This is how we build walls of defense around our lives and destiny. We budget for all the gates of our government so that every gate receives an allocation according to our objectives.

- **He Gave**

Jesus gave out the resources. The key word here is 'giving.' It is a moral obligation that we give to the poor, strangers and disenfranchised in society. We do not invest in this category of people in the technical sense but as a moral responsibility. You cannot invest in a stranger because there is no established relationship that secures the investment. "My son, if thou be surety for thy friend, if thou hast stricken thy hand with a stranger, Thou art snared with the words of thy mouth, thou art taken with the words of thy mouth. Do this now, my son, and deliver thyself, when thou art come into the hand of thy friend; go, humble thyself, and make sure thy friend. Give not sleep to thine eyes, nor slumber to thine eyelids. Deliver thyself as a roe from the hand of the hunter, and as a bird from the hand of the fowler" Proverbs 6:1-5.

Your contacts with strangers are casual and the relationship is superficial. You can help a stranger or any human being based on their needs for survival. It is not wise to entrust your capital resources as investment with people with whom you do not have a solid relationship. The poor, strangers and disenfranchised in society are a part of God's way of calibrating our timing to resonate with divinely orchestrated opportunities.

Once I was on my way to Dallas from Heathrow Airport in London, UK and I had to switch flights at JFK in New York. There was this old lady travelling to Connecticut in the United States and the flight we were about to board was to JFK New York. The flight check-in crew made an appeal for any passenger that would want to assist the old lady through the flight. I immediately perceived this as a divine opportunity so volunteered. When we arrived at JFK Airport, there were several aircrafts that had arrived simultaneously so the queue through immigration and customs was exceeding long. The son of this old lady was meeting her at JFK so he arranged for her to be picked up from the gangway with a wheel chair. The official who came for the old lady noticed I was her help so she advised me to stay by her side. This way, we bypassed the long queue and within minutes I was out. My connecting flight from JFK to Dallas was almost due at this time and assuming I was to go through the queue of immigration and customs, I would have missed the flight to Dallas. You can imagine the inconvenience! Though it may have seemed as though this old lady would have been a drag on my swift progress through the journey, helping her recalibrated my timing!

Manifestation Plan

Chapter
Three

POST-MANIFESTATION ERA

" A nd the seven years of plenteousness, that was in the land of Egypt, were ended. And the seven years of dearth began to come, according as Joseph had said: and the dearth was in all lands; but in all the land of Egypt there was bread. And when all the land of Egypt was famished, the people cried to Pharaoh for bread: and Pharaoh said unto all the Egyptians, Go unto Joseph; what he saith to you, do. And the famine was over all the face of the earth: and Joseph opened all the storehouses, and sold unto the Egyptians; and the famine waxed sore in the land of Egypt. And all countries came into Egypt to Joseph for to buy corn; because that the famine was so sore in all lands" Genesis 41:53-57.

For seven years, Joseph executed his plan of investing in the corn of the Egyptians. During this period of abundance, I believe there were several people who ridiculed the wisdom of Joseph investing in corn. It was so abundant that with economic laws of demand and supply in play, corn would have become so cheap in value. However, when the seven year period of abundance came to an end, the drought began to manifest as Joseph had foretold.

In Isaiah 32 we see the contrast of an era of abundance as against an environment of famine. "See, a king will reign in righteousness and rulers will rule with justice. Each one will be like a shelter from the wind and a refuge from the storm, like streams of water in the desert and the shadow of a great rock in a thirsty land. Then the eyes of those who see will no longer be closed, and the ears of those who hear will listen. The fearful heart will know and understand, and the stammering tongue will be fluent and clear. No longer will the fool be called noble nor the scoundrel be highly respected. For fools speak folly, their hearts are bent on evil: They practice ungodliness and spread error concerning the LORD; the hungry they leave empty and from the thirsty they withhold water. Scoundrels use wicked methods, they make up evil schemes to destroy the poor with lies, even when the plea of the needy is just. But the noble make noble plans, and by noble deeds they stand. You women who are so complacent, rise up and listen to me; you daughters who feel secure, hear what I have to say! In little more than a year you who feel secure will tremble; the grape harvest will fail, and the harvest of fruit will not come. Tremble, you complacent women; shudder, you daughters who feel secure! Strip off your fine clothes and wrap yourselves in rags. Beat your breasts for the pleasant fields, for the fruitful vines and for the land of my people, a land overgrown with thorns and briers—yes, mourn for all houses of merriment and for this city of revelry. The fortress will be abandoned, the noisy city deserted; citadel and watchtower will become a wasteland forever, the delight of donkeys, a pasture for flocks, till the Spirit is poured on us from on high, and the desert becomes a fertile field, and the fertile field seems like a forest. The LORD's justice will dwell in the desert, his righteousness live in the fertile field. The fruit of that righteousness will be peace; its effect will be quietness and confidence forever. My people will live in peaceful dwelling places, in secure homes, in undisturbed places of rest. Though hail flattens the forest and the city is leveled completely, how blessed you will be, sowing your seed by every stream, and letting your cattle and donkeys range free."

An era of famine is when the grace of righteousness is withheld from above. Satan fills the gap and wickedness becomes predominant in society. "The wicked walk on every side, when the vilest men are exalted" Psalm 12:8. Whenever corruption becomes the celebrated way of advancing our aspirations, it is evidence of drought. Society degenerates and life becomes sour for people of noble minds. During a drought the mantra of life is always 'survival of the fittest.' The 'fittest' are those who are able to conform to the vices of the day. In such times, those in authority usually exploit others to amass riches.

THE STOREHOUSES OF WISDOM

The Egyptians cried to Pharaoh for bread and he directed them to go to Joseph. Joseph had kept the corn in storehouses from which he sold corn to the Egyptians. Everyone who came to Joseph to procure corn came with a unique need. They came because there was a drought, which means no supply from heaven. The need of the architect is different from that of a tailor and the need of a farmer is different from the blacksmith. They all came to Joseph because they could not flourish in their vocations. Heaven had held back whatever made them prosperous. However, one man had it all. Joseph had invested into what would bring people sustenance during the seven years of famine he had predicted courtesy of the Pharaoh's dream. Joseph built the storehouses based on the wisdom of God.

"Wisdom hath builded her house, she hath hewn out her seven pillars: She hath killed her beasts; she hath mingled her wine; she hath also furnished her table. She hath sent forth her maidens: she crieth upon the highest places of the city, Whoso is simple, let him turn in hither: as for him that wanteth understanding, she saith to him, Come, eat of my bread, and drink of the wine which I have mingled. Forsake the foolish, and live; and go in the way of understanding" Proverbs 9:1-6.

Wisdom builds her house on seven pillars. She furnishes food to all who seek understanding. Joseph had invested into the Egyptians during the seven years of abundance. Now it was time to liquidate! During the seven years of abundance Joseph built storehouses on the foundation of seven. Seven is the protocol of God's house. There were seven core objects of fellowship in the tabernacle of God which was revealed to Moses. The revelation from these seven objects of fellowship unfolds the mysteries of divine providence.

1. THE BRAZEN LAVER STOREHOUSE

This object of fellowship was a water basin, made of high polished brass that gave a mirror-like reflection of the worshipper. As a first step of fellowship, the worshipper would take water from the brazen laver to wash their hands and feet. Our hands signify our works and our feet signify our ways. At this point in our fellowship, we reflect on our works and ways, seeking to align ourselves with the standards of God's word. "The words of the LORD are pure words: as silver tried in a furnace of earth, purified seven times" Psalm 12:6.

God's word is the divine standard for all skill and excellence. The ultimate perfection of who we are and mastery of what we are called to be is only attainable through God's word.

"All scripture is given by inspiration of God, and is profitable for doctrine, for reproof, for correction, for instruction in righteousness: That the man of God may be perfect, thoroughly furnished unto all good works" 2 Timothy 3:16&17.

Instruction in righteousness, doctrines, correction, reproof are the sequence of how God's word brings us into divine skill and excellence. Instruction in righteousness is when we study the scriptures to acquire a broad understanding of God's word. Doctrines are teachings based on specific spiritual subjects like sin, eternal life, angels etc. Correction is to call our attention to measure up to the standards of God's word when we are wrong. Reproof is to apply some disciplinary measure when we repeatedly act contrary to scriptures in areas where we have been corrected in the past. These processes of God's word purge us of the nature of evil. Inherent evil robs us of the ability to manifest our divine attributes. God's word empowers us to restore the original image and likeness of God in us.

- **Divine Values and Burdens**

God's word is the source of divine values. Divine values saddle us with divine burdens that guide our creativity as humans. Without divine values our aspirations and creativity tends towards self-aggrandizement and ultimately a culture of oppressiveness. Some corporate enterprises in our society today prey on people and seek only to profiteer in all their goals.

"Help, LORD; for the godly man ceaseth; for the faithful fail from among the children of men. They speak vanity every one with his neighbour: with flattering lips and with a double heart do they speak.

The LORD shall cut off all flattering lips, and the tongue that speaketh proud things: Who have said, With our tongue will we prevail; our lips are our own: who is lord over us? For the oppression of the poor, for the sighing of the needy, now will I arise, saith the LORD; I will set him in safety from him that puffeth at him. The words of the LORD are pure words: as silver tried in a furnace of earth, purified seven times. Thou shalt keep them, O LORD, thou shalt preserve them from this generation for ever. The wicked walk on every side, when the vilest men are exalted" Psalm 12.

When God looks out of heaven, He sees the oppression of mankind and hears the cries of the poor. A universal lifestyle of oppression also results in the earth turning a corner away from God's grand plan and so divine correction becomes necessary. Throughout the scriptures we encounter the ministry of prophets who were sent to warn Israel so that nation experienced times of divine correction. Noah warned his generation of unrighteousness before the flood that came as judgment and wiped out those who were not with him in the ark. Jonah the prophet was sent by God to warn Nineveh which was a non-Jewish city to change from their ways to avert the consequences of reproof which comes as an act of judgment. Sodom and Gomorrah was judged by God and destroyed by fire because of the wickedness of the inhabitants.

Throughout the scriptures we find instances where individuals, rulers and communities are subjected to divine judgment and are either promoted, demoted or even destroyed. King Nebuchadnezzar was subjected to divine judgment and when found guilty of arrogance; he was sentenced to live as a beast for seven years until he acknowledged that God was the ultimate ruler of heaven and earth. He was restored to his throne and continued his reign. King Nebuchadnezzar's son King Belshazzar who inherited the kingdom was also subjected to divine judgment, when he drank from the vessels of God's house. The scripture says "He was weighed in the balances and found wanting." He was judged guilty, lost the throne and was killed.

Usually God will send prophets to warn those who are being judged to measure up to the standards of His word. Assuming that they respond and start to apply divine values to their ways, correction is achieved so there is no need for rebuke or punishment. However if they refuse to heed correction, then the rebuke of punishment is dispensed.

- ## Self Correction and Rebuke

The reason we must be instructed in righteousness and doctrine is to establish the inherent ability for self-correction and self-rebuke. "But he that is spiritual judgeth all things, yet he himself is judged of no man" 1 Corinthians 2:15. If we have the standards by which God judges us in our conscience, then we might as well self-correct when we identify that we fall short of God's values. This way we avert the judgment of punishment.

"But in a great house there are not only vessels of gold and of silver, but also of wood and of earth; and some to honor, and some to dishonor. If a man therefore purge himself from these, he shall be a vessel unto honor, sanctified, and meet for the master's use, and prepared unto every good work" 2 Timothy 2:20&21.

The elements mentioned here, gold, silver, wood and earth all reflect our diversity in divine potentials. However we get classified as either a vessel of honor or dishonor based on our level of refinement. The scripture goes on to say: "if a man therefore purge himself of these, he shall be a vessel unto honor, sanctified and meet for the master's use." The responsibility of purging our potentials from impurities lies within us. No spiritual leader or teacher is responsible for purging us. Spiritual leaders facilitate us with the revelation of God's word but then the onus lies upon us to apply revelation to our lives.

- **Education versus Transformation**

Most often as New Testament believers, we tend to receive revelation like secular education. Acquiring secular education is entirely a mental process where we are taught or we study a curriculum to become proficient in a vocation. We learn the history of that vocation and current practices to be able to function in that area of endeavoring. This process of education is entirely different from transformation. Transformation is the process of change that God's word is intended to accomplish in us.

"But after that the kindness and love of God our Savior toward man appeared, Not by works of righteousness which we have done, but according to his mercy he saved us, by the washing of regeneration, and renewing of the Holy Ghost; Which he shed on us abundantly through Jesus Christ our Saviour; That being justified by his grace, we should be made heirs according to the hope of eternal life" Titus 3:4-7.

The scripture uses the phrase 'washing of regeneration' to describe the transformation process of salvation. Washing is the water-effect of God's word on us. It cleanses our minds of vices that we have learned from wrong sources. Regeneration is the process where we are reconfigured to function contrary to the deplorable trends of our generation. God's word impacts us through conviction. When we are in the atmosphere where God's word is taught, our attitude is to become open to conviction. Conviction is how divine truth arrests our hearts so that we are left with no other option but to apply ourselves to these truths. When we apply ourselves to function by divine truths, we become one with truth. In John 1:14, the scripture describes the lifestyle of Jesus: "And the Word was made flesh, and dwelt among us, (and we beheld his glory, the glory as of the only begotten of the Father,) full of grace and truth." The Word becomes flesh when we apply ourselves to divine truth that convicts us. God's word manifests His glory so when we act on divine truths we become the manifestation of God's glory here on earth. Yielding ourselves to function in divine conviction unveils honor and the excellence of God in us.

During the process of creating the heavens and the earth, the scripture says that God always qualified His work as 'good.' The word 'good' also means virtue and excellent. Good, virtue and excellence is the life of God accomplished in us through the transformation of divine truth. Though divine truth is stored in the conscience of our minds, it is not intended as education is, to be only head knowledge. While you can pass a school test by answering questions correctly from your memory, a spiritual test of your degree of transformation is how you react to situations that require your application and perseverance with divine truth. Divine truth is the conscience of our spirit, soul and body. It is the first pillar of our entire existence. The transformation of divine truth determines the level of honor in us. Such honor is how we measure up to divine values. It is our level of purity. While education is our worth to fellow man, transformation is our worth in the sight of God.

- **Money fails in Egypt**

The seven years of famine begun and when the Egyptians went to Pharaoh about the lack of food, he tells them: "Go unto Joseph; what he saith to you, do." The Pharaoh could have simply said: "Go to the storehouses and buy food." The needs of the people were not as simple as that. They were all involved in various vocations and the famine challenged them in different ways. During the seven years of abundance, Joseph invested in their corn based on their distinct vocations. For instance, the corn of the wheat farmer was different from the corn of the potato farmer. This means that during the famine, their individual needs were different.

Joseph asks them to bring money for their sustenance. When you think of a famine in today's context, we commonly say there is an economic hardship. Every industry struggles to survive. The problem of an economic depression is not typically food because in a global environment, we can get fresh vegetables grown in Japan, here in America within two days of its harvest. The sustenance of the farmer is different from that of an architect. This is why the Pharaoh of Egypt instructs his people to go to Joseph and obey whatever he tells them to do. Everyone lined up to see Joseph for their peculiar challenges.

The medium of exchange was gold. In economics, anything that is considered money must have the qualities of standard of value, measure of value and store of value. Notice the words 'Standard', 'Measure' and 'Store', as well as 'Value.' These words describe the attributes of God's word and so let me incorporate these words in one statement: 'The standard by which God measures our lives to determine if we have the values of eternity is His word.' God's word is the 'true gold.'

The purpose of the Brazen laver is to facilitate us to get rid of the impurities of our works and ways. These impurities are classified in the scriptures as: Darkness, Ignorance, Failure, Leprosy, Lameness, Spots, Blemish and Wrinkles. Sanctification is the process where God's word like water, washes us of all such vices. When the vices are removed, the true values of God's word become unveiled through our transformed way of life. The 'true gold' emerges in our works and ways as the real value of our lives. The transformed life is our worth in the eyes of God.

Education is necessary to equip everyone with the history and current practices of a vocation. However it is only God's word that has the power to transform us to line up with God's plan of the future of our lives. Our creative skills emerge only when God's values become our values. For instance an automobile engineer learns from college the up-to-date practice of auto engineering. He is certified and can work in any vehicle manufacturing company and earn an income. His income is the value placed on his education and experience. The future of the company where he works depends on if they remain competitive in their vehicle products. Assuming other competitors roll out better vehicles, more people will patronize these vehicles. This means that the company where this automobile engineer works will continue to lose their share of the market unless they come up with great designs. Assuming they are not able to come up with competitive designs, they will experience economic hardships and start to lay off workers. All the businesses connected with this auto company such as clients and customers will be affected and may start experiencing the same hardship and consequences.

Remember that the root of the problem is the inability to come up with creative designs that make them competitive. Assuming this auto engineer becomes aware that he might lose his job soon, he knows the consequence of no-pay-check. He comes to Joseph and lays out his problem. Joseph discerns that the absence of creative skills is the root and so the brazen laver storehouse is where this auto engineer will be furnished to go and design competitive vehicles.

- **The Convergence of Education and Transformation**

Education without transformation may bring the efforts of a particular generation to a grinding halt or economic drought while transformation without education means there is no legacy inherited. Both education and transformation are necessary to work alongside each other. Many businesses attempt to project into the future by establishing a research and development department. The research and development department is simply an extension of the impact of education but can never make up for the impact of transformation. The future is the direction where God intends for the entire earth. The generational goals of God are all enshrined in divine values. The transformation of divine values lays unique burdens of those who belong to a generation. This is the essence of regeneration.

In our previous assumption, Joseph gives the auto engineer a signed slip to go to the brazen laver storehouse for supplies. Joseph discerned that this auto engineer needed an encounter that activates his creative skills. Let us get a little more practical here. Many road accidents today are as a result of blind spots around most vehicles owing to their design. The rear-view and side mirrors of most vehicles are not able to capture these blind spots so vehicles changing lanes on a highway end up crashing into others in their blind spot. Though a simple technology that captures the blind spot of a vehicle may only add a little to the cost of making a vehicle, many corporations are administered to be more cost efficient and profit sensitive so safety is least of their concerns. There is a principle of scripture that requires that in building a house, the builder should incorporate safety features so people do not become victims of death. "When thou buildest a new house, then thou shalt make a battlement for thy roof, that thou bring not blood upon thine house, if any man fall from thence" Deuteronomy 22:8. At the brazen laver storehouse, this auto engineer is transformed by this scripture to place safety over profit so he becomes burdened to incorporate the blind spot safety feature into the design of vehicles. That becomes a new selling point as consumers may gravitate towards this brand for the new safety features. Divine values place divine burdens at the forefront of our hearts to guide and enhance our creative skills as well as our quest for excellence.

Like the currencies commonly used as money today, education is our fiduciary or face value and together with transformation, we achieve our full intrinsic or real value. The real worth of a man is the sum of his education and transformation.

• **Our Conscience and Intuition**

The conscience is that aspect of our soul that holds our intuition for distinguishing right from wrong. Think of yourself standing in front of this water basin that gives a reflection of your image. The water in this basin is able to wash away every impurity from your body and make you clean to the degree you desire. Let us think of the brazen laver as the conscience of our soul, while the water it holds as our intuition. The brazen laver like our conscience is an inherent mirror while the water is intuition, which facilitates the values of our transformation.

Intuition is how God unveils His works to our soul. As we share in His values, our conscience picks up the reflection of God's works so we can mirror

His excellence and creative attributes. "Then answered Jesus and said unto them, Verily, verily, I say unto you, The Son can do nothing of himself, but what he seeth the Father do: for what things soever he doeth, these also doeth the Son likewise" John 5:19.

Sin clouds our conscience with spots, wrinkles and blemishes. The laver holds water which is God's word that is able to sanctify our souls from spiritual spots, wrinkles and blemish. In the Old Testament era, if a worshipper brought an animal to be offered as a sacrifice, the Levites will first examine it to determine there were no spots, wrinkles or blemishes. Spot, wrinkle and blemish disqualified animals to be used as sacrifice. They were an indication of sin. The worshipper was seeking atonement from sin so they had to present an animal that had no appearance of sin as an offering. Jesus Christ qualified as the perfect sacrifice for all humanity. "Who did no sin, neither was guile found in his mouth" 1 Peter 2:22.

The function of the brazen laver was to help us overcome the nature of sin through the conviction of the word. Spot, wrinkle and blemish on a mirror will certainly distort the image of whoever stands before it. The Apostle Paul describes people with a distorted conscience, "Speaking lies in hypocrisy; having their conscience seared with a hot iron" 1 Timothy 4:2. To understand how the conscience works, we have to think of a mirror in its perfect form and what would happen if someone takes a hot iron and smacks it.

The mirror becomes cracked and would not provide a perfect reflection of things in its view. This is what happens when people continually defy their conscience. The conscience becomes wacked so it gets confused as to the difference between right and wrong. To keep ones conscience from being wacked, we must stay true to the values of our transformation at all times.

• Convictions of the Conscience

The Apostle John records an interesting encounter between Jesus and scribes: "And the scribes and Pharisees brought unto him a woman taken in adultery; and when they had set her in the midst, They say unto him, Master, this woman was taken in adultery, in the very act. Now Moses in the law commanded us, that such should be stoned: but what sayest thou? This they said, tempting him that they might have to accuse him. But Jesus stooped down, and with his finger wrote on the ground, as though he heard them not. So when they continued asking him, he lifted up himself, and said unto them, He that is without sin among you, let him first cast a stone at her. And again he stooped down, and wrote on the ground. And they which heard it, being convicted by their own conscience, went out one by one, beginning at the eldest, even unto the last: and Jesus was left alone, and the woman standing in the midst. When Jesus had lifted up himself, and saw none but the woman, he said unto her, Woman, where are those thine accusers? hath no man condemned thee? She said, No man, Lord. And Jesus said unto her, Neither do I condemn thee: go, and sin no more" John 8:3-11.

This story leaves us with two fundamental questions. First of all, where is the man who was involved with the woman in adultery? It takes two to be involved in such a violation of the commandments, so it would be logical that the man should also be arrested together with the woman. That was evidence of hypocrisy of these scribes and Pharisees. They subjected the woman and the man to a different standard of judgment which was not fair.

The second question is: If they felt justified by the commandment to lynch this woman, why did they bother to seek the opinion of Jesus first? It was obvious that this woman was guilty of the Law of Moses and so in the past, those who violated this law were quickly punished. However, since the advent of the ministry of Jesus, a new standard had been set. The Apostle Peter puts it this way: "How God anointed Jesus of Nazareth with the Holy Ghost and with power: who went about doing good, and healing all that were oppressed of the devil; for God was with him" Acts 10:38. A new standard of good had been set for Israel by the ministry of Jesus. His teachings unveiled the mysteries of God's word and made them relevant by the demonstration of power that confirmed these truths.

If we compare the impact of the religious leaders with the ministry of Jesus, it was like night and day. The religious leaders were holding the masses to a standard that they secretly violated in their personal lives. The reason they brought this woman to Jesus was that they did not feel at ease with the punishment they were about to discharge on this woman. The ministry of Jesus had become the new brazen laver of society. His teachings and impact had become the new conscience of the day. The religious leaders were now measuring their intentions with this new standard.

Though one of their motives was to entangle Jesus with this woman caught in adultery and to make him equally guilty if He was in discord with the Law of Moses, for once they were not sure whether lynching the woman qualified as good or wrong. Jesus answers them in the most astounding way: "He that is without sin among you, let him first cast a stone at her." Wow! Jesus implies that He is not in discord with the Law of Moses. However it is important that they all measure themselves to the same standard. If this woman is guilty and deserves to die, let whoever does not deserve to die be the first to discharge judgment on her. In other words Jesus was saying: "Let everyone look at themselves in their own mirrors." The impact is profound as these religious leaders 'convicted by their conscience' started departing from the scene until there is none left. Jesus tells the woman what should radically transform her: "Neither do I condemn thee: go, and sin no more." In other words, 'You just had a close encounter with death, you have another chance at life and so measure up to the standard of righteousness.' When the brazen laver of our conscience is filled with pure water, we can wash ourselves of whatever defiles us so that we are able to mirror the excellence and creative attributes of God.

2. ALTAR OF SACRIFICE STOREHOUSE

As the famine in Egypt continued unabated, the people run out of money. They came to Joseph and complained they had no money to buy food and he told them to bring their cattle in exchange for food. In most heathen cultures, animals and their blood were offered as sacrifices to gods. If Joseph required their cattle in exchange for food, this would ultimately deprive them of the capability of offering animal and blood sacrifices to their gods. At this point, they would have realized that their gods could not help them anyway. Whatever Joseph required from them was the key to their sustenance.

In the Old Testament era of Israel's history, animal sacrifices were offered on the Altar of Sacrifice and the blood made atonement for the soul. This is significant of the place where Jesus Christ was crucified on the cross at Calvary. Jesus Christ is the Lamb of God that makes atonement for our souls. "In whom we have redemption through his blood, the forgiveness of sins, according to the riches of his grace" Ephesians 1:7. Several core New Testament era words such as salvation and deliverance underscore the essence of redemption. Redemption means to be bought back from the consequences of sin. Many problems that we face as humans are direct consequences of sin.

"For all have sinned, and come short of the glory of God" Romans 3:23. "For the wages of sin is death; but the gift of God is eternal life through Jesus Christ our Lord" Romans 6:23. Sin is a trap that holds people bound up in infirmities as well as various forms of spiritual, emotional, mental, financial and physical captivity. When we fall into the trap of sin, it denies us access to the fullness of God's goodness. To enjoy the fullness of God's goodness, we need redemption from the trappings of sin.

The people in Joseph's era needed to be emancipated from the famine and Joseph had the key to their deliverance from imminent starvation. Their sustenance was held in a storehouse Joseph had labeled as the Altar of Sacrifice Storehouse. The impact of this famine was beyond Egypt and Joseph's brothers came to buy food from Egypt. They appeared before Joseph who recognized them immediately but they did not recognize him. In their minds, Joseph was dead because that was the sentence they handed him several years ago. Joseph spoke to them through an interpreter so they had no clue he was their blood brother. He accused them of being spies as a way of getting them to divulge information about the state of affairs of the family and Jacob their father. They mentioned Benjamin their kid brother and Joseph required them to dispatch one person to fetch him as evidence that they were not spies. Nine of them would be held in prison until Benjamin is brought to Egypt. At this point these ten brothers are unraveled. "And they said one to another, We are verily guilty concerning our brother, in that we saw the anguish of his soul, when he besought us, and we would not hear; therefore is this distress come upon us. And Reuben answered them, saying, Spake I not unto you, saying, Do not sin against the child; and ye would not hear? therefore, behold, also his blood is required" Genesis 42:21&22.

Though they had buried Joseph in their minds, this circumstance that confronted them immediately reminded them of their sinful act to Joseph. Not knowing that Joseph understood what they were saying, they confessed their sins before him. Reuben makes a profound statement: "behold, also his blood is required." Joseph's requirement for Benjamin to be brought to Egypt as proof that they were not spies was like pulling a tooth. Benjamin was the last born and their father Jacob loved him so much. Furthermore, Rachel had died at his birth and as far as Jacob knew, Joseph was also dead. In the minds of these ten brothers, Benjamin whom Jacob may never let go, is now required of them as an object of atonement.

After holding these ten brothers for three days in a prison, Joseph makes a deal with them. "And Joseph said unto them the third day, This do, and live;

for I fear God: If ye be true men, let one of your brethren be bound in the house of your prison: go ye, carry corn for the famine of your houses: But bring your youngest brother unto me; so shall your words be verified, and ye shall not die. And they did so" Genesis 42:18-20. Simeon was chosen to stay in prison while the other nine brothers went back to Canaan to fetch Benjamin.

- **Anatomy of Sin**

Sin is a debt. Transgression, Trespass and Iniquity are words used to describe various kinds of sin in the scriptures. Technically, transgression is to violate the principles of God's word. It is a sin directed at God. Typically, trespass is a violation of mankind. It is sin against our fellow man. Iniquity simply means wickedness. It is intentional evil. If you pay careful attention to the Ten Commandments, which are a summary of God's commandments, you will notice that while some are directed towards our relationship with God, others target human relations.

Regardless of whether our sin is a transgression, trespass or iniquity, there are consequences of spiritual, emotional, financial or physical debts. In the Old Testament era, those who could not pay up their debts were held as bond servants. They worked for their creditors to pay up the debts. Similarly, in the spiritual realm, debts are not swept under the carpet as if they do not exist. The evidence of spiritual sins sometimes manifests as incurable infirmities, plagues and unexplainable limitations.

There is an interesting story in the scriptures of how King Saul trespassed against the Gibeonites and the consequences Israel experienced. "Then there was a famine in the days of David three years, year after year; and David enquired of the LORD. And the LORD answered, It is for Saul, and for his bloody house, because he slew the Gibeonites. And the king called the Gibeonites, and said unto them; (now the Gibeonites were not of the children of Israel, but of the remnant of the Amorites; and the children of Israel had sworn unto them: and Saul sought to slay them in his zeal to the children of Israel and Judah.) Wherefore David said unto the Gibeonites, What shall I do for you? and wherewith shall I make the atonement, that ye may bless the inheritance of the LORD? And the Gibeonites said unto him, We will have no silver nor gold of Saul, nor of his house; neither for us shalt thou kill any man in Israel. And he said, What ye shall say, that will I do for you. And they answered the king, The man that consumed us, and that devised against us that we should be destroyed from remaining in any of the coasts of Israel, Let seven men of his sons be delivered unto us, and we will hang them up unto the LORD in Gibeah of Saul, whom the LORD did choose. And the king said, I will give them" 2 Samuel 21:1-6.

It is interesting that when King David seeks God about the persistent famine, God diagnoses the

117

problem but offers King David no direct solution. God directs King David to the Gibeonites against whom Israel has committed a trespass. The plague of famine came to an end when Israel fulfilled the request of the Gibeonites.

There is a strange teaching in some Christian circles today that implies that because of grace, there is no more consequence for sins. To such people the Apostle Paul asks a question in Romans 6:1: "What shall we say then? Shall we continue in sin, that grace may abound?" While grace is the unmerited favor of God that ends the era of animal sacrifices for the atonement of sins, grace does not mean that we are not held accountable for our sins. To enjoy the gift of grace, we have to first repent from our sins and then invoke the grace of God through the blood of Jesus.

Repentance is the first step in the protocol for approaching God. Sanctification through repentance is what took place at the Brazen Laver which was the first object of worship in the tabernacle of Moses. Consecration came second. Consecration means to be dedicated to God through sacrifice. The impact of blood sacrifice comes after sanctification. The washing of water comes first and it is followed by the consecration of blood. Without repentance there can be no real forgiveness of sins.

I know what you may be thinking right now. How about the scriptures that say: "Blessed are they whose iniquities are forgiven, and whose sins are covered. Blessed is the man to whom the Lord will not impute sin" Romans 4:7&8. The work of grace is the sacrifice of Jesus Christ for us on the cross of Calvary. This means that before any of us was involved in any sin, Jesus Christ had already paid the price for our forgiveness. Grace is available for us all to tap into, first by believing in the grace of our Lord Jesus Christ and then secondly by confession of our sins.

"But the righteousness which is of faith speaketh on this wise, Say not in thine heart, Who shall ascend into heaven? (that is, to bring Christ down from above:) Or, Who shall descend into the deep? (that is, to bring up Christ again from the dead.) But what saith it? The word is nigh thee, even in thy mouth, and in thy heart: that is, the word of faith, which we preach; That if thou shalt confess with thy mouth the Lord Jesus, and shalt believe in thine heart that God hath raised him from the dead, thou shalt be saved. For with the heart man believeth unto righteousness; and with the mouth confession is made unto salvation. For the scripture saith, Whosoever believeth on him shall not be ashamed. For there is no difference between the Jew and the Greek: for the same Lord over all is rich unto all that call upon him. For whosoever shall call upon the name of the Lord shall be saved" Romans 10:6-13. Throughout the book of Romans, the Apostle Paul is up against those who were distorting the message about the grace of our Lord Jesus Christ, and so he brings the process of grace into perspective:

First of all, 'believe' in the message of our Lord Jesus Christ leads one to repentance, which is a change of heart that tends to righteousness. When someone believes in the gospel of our Lord Jesus Christ, the evidence of their believe manifests as a change of heart towards a life of sin. This is what is known as the righteousness of God and in the Old Testament it was a function of the Brazen Laver where worshipers were sanctified as a first step.

Secondly, confessing Jesus Christ as Lord brings the work of the cross to bear upon such a person and produces salvation. In the Old Testament, the worshiper would lay hands on the animal and confessed their sins before it was offered at the Altar of sacrifice. The Apostle John brings this act into New Testament relevance: "If we confess our sins, he is faithful and just to forgive us our sins, and to cleanse us from all unrighteousness. If we say that we have not sinned, we make him a liar, and his word is not in us" 1 John 1:9&10. Confession is the prerequisite to salvation. Confession is to admit our faults and seek forgiveness through the blood of Jesus.

Grace therefore is not a license to sin; rather it is the gift of God that gives us access to the redeeming power of the blood of Jesus Christ. This grace has been lavished upon our dispensation so that though we are forgiven even before we commit sin, we have to tap into this grace through believe and confession.

In the same way Joseph had to deal with the sins of the Egyptians which were not atoned for and so they became victims of a famine, the Apostle Paul had to deal with a generation that wanted to take grace for granted. Unfortunately, today's generation of New Testament believers are caught in this same trap and so the awesome deliverance and healing power of God is limited in our lives.

- ## Intercession and Forgiveness

The entire chapter of Isaiah 53 unveils the revelation of intercession and its relationship with deliverance and healing. "Who hath believed our report? and to whom is the arm of the LORD revealed? For he shall grow up before him as a tender plant, and as a root out of a dry ground: he hath no form nor comeliness; and when we shall see him, there is no beauty that we should desire him. He is despised and rejected of men; a man of sorrows, and acquainted with grief: and we hid as it were our faces from him; he was despised, and we esteemed him not. Surely he hath borne our griefs, and carried our sorrows: yet we did esteem him stricken, smitten of God, and afflicted. But he was wounded for our transgressions, he was bruised for our iniquities: the chastisement of our peace was upon him; and with his stripes we are healed. All we like sheep have gone astray; we have turned every one to his own way; and the LORD hath laid on him the iniquity of us all. He was oppressed, and he was afflicted, yet he opened not his mouth: he is brought as a lamb to the slaughter, and as a sheep before her shearers is dumb, so he openeth not his mouth. He was taken from prison and from judgment: and who shall declare his generation? for he was cut off out of the land of the living: for the transgression of my people was he stricken. And he made his grave with the wicked, and with the rich in his death; because he had done no violence, neither was any deceit in his mouth. Yet it pleased the LORD to bruise him; he hath put him to grief: when thou shalt make his soul an offering for sin, he shall see his seed, he shall prolong his days, and the pleasure of the LORD shall prosper in his hand. He shall see of the travail of his soul, and shall be satisfied: by his knowledge shall my righteous servant justify many; for he shall bear their iniquities. Therefore will I divide him a portion with the great, and he shall divide the spoil with the strong; because he hath poured out his soul unto death: and he was numbered with the transgressors; and he bare the sin of many, and made intercession for the transgressors."

This scripture was a prophetic word that describes the intercessory ministry of our Lord Jesus Christ. Intercession is to stand in the gap for others. Intercession builds a bridge between the earth and heaven, sinners and God. The intercessor is like the animal that was offered in sacrifice to God. For no fault of the animal, it is offered to make atonement for the sins of its owner. In the same way, the intercessor would be required to pay for the sins of others. In the case of an intercessor, the burden of sins is borne in advance. Through the divine arrangement of God, Jesus was made to suffer for sins He did not commit. This way, Jesus accumulated a credit in the heavenly bank of God. From this credit He makes withdrawals to atone for our sins whenever we seek forgiveness through the blood of Jesus.

The intercession of Christ for us works through the dynamics of forgiveness. "For if ye forgive men their trespasses, your heavenly Father will also forgive you: But if ye forgive not men their trespasses, neither will your Father forgive your trespasses" Matthew 6:14&15. The requirement for us to forgive those who trespass against us is a dynamic that recruits us into intercession. Notice that by intercession, Jesus was wounded for our transgression and bruised for our iniquities. In the same way, those we are required to forgive are those who have hurt us. We are required to forgive them and not seek vengeance against them. This way we stand in the gap for them and prevent the judgment of God against them.

- **Demonic Mandates**

Commonly known as curses, demonic mandates are the license for evil spirits to act against a person, place or things. Demonic mandates can either be established by occultists or whenever man becomes a victim of sin. In God's original design, man is blessed with dominion over creation. The fall of Adam and

Eve in the Garden of Eden to the vice of sin is the reason for the loss of man's dominion. Some sicknesses, diseases, inhibitions, bondages and captivity may be manifestations of curses.

"Then I turned, and lifted up mine eyes, and looked, and behold a flying roll. And he said unto me, What seest thou? And I answered, I see a flying roll; the length thereof is twenty cubits, and the breadth thereof ten cubits. Then said he unto me, This is the curse that goeth forth over the face of the whole earth: for every one that stealeth shall be cut off as on this side according to it; and every one that sweareth shall be cut off as on that side according to it. I will bring it forth, saith the LORD of hosts, and it shall enter into the house of the thief, and into the house of him that sweareth falsely by my name: and it shall remain in the midst of his house, and shall consume it with the timber thereof and the stones thereof" Zechariah 5:1-4.

A man's sins are inscribed on a flying scroll that hovers over them. These sins become an open mandate for evil spirits to discharge punishment. There are so many people going through unexplainable conditions of life which may be as a result of the flying scroll hovering over their lives.

- **Healing and Deliverance**

The cross is where Jesus paid the price for our healing and deliverance. Through intercession, He makes the case for our redemption from the trappings of sin.

Most of the manifestations of infirmities and unusual barriers and limitations we experience are the direct consequence of sins. At the cross, Jesus dealt with all curses, sicknesses, diseases and bondages associated with sin.

Many healing ministries today have discovered that the relationship between intercession, forgiveness, healing and deliverance is so inexcusable. They are strongly linked such that they work together. To experience healing and deliverance in most cases, there must be intercession and forgiveness. Based on this insight, several healing ministries hold healing classes to establish this understanding with those seeking healing as part of the process to foster greater results.

- **Emotions and Discernment**

The emotion is an aspect of the soul that relates to our feelings. Usually we all have the power to control how we feel and relate to our environment. In some cases however, we find ourselves incapable of controlling our feelings and are unusually overwhelmed by lust so that we do those things which we have repented and resolved never to do again. The roots of certain overwhelming lusts are bloodline related. That means they are like eggs in the bloodline. Let us consider two subsequent generations of one family. Assuming the first generation of this family unit endeavors to apply their convictions of God's word to their lives to the best of their ability, the next generation will not inherit any eggs of vices in their bloodline.

However, un-confessed sins and unresolved curses from one generation may pass on to the next generation as eggs in the bloodline. "Let no man say when he is tempted, I am tempted of God: for God cannot be tempted with evil, neither tempteth he any man: But every man is tempted, when he is drawn away of his own lust, and enticed. Then when lust hath conceived, it bringeth forth sin: and sin, when it is finished, bringeth forth death" James 1:13-15. The enemy identifies these eggs in the bloodline and lures the victim through temptation. When the tempter encounters the eggs of lust within the victim there is conception and the victim of such a spiritual operation cannot resist the temptation to sin. Such people who find themselves unable to live a life of righteousness are under bondage and need supernatural freedom. We often classify such people as being emotionally unstable because they have no control over their desires. To change this condition, the blood of Jesus is invoked to effect deliverance by purging this bloodline.

To maintain victory over the tempter, we need to operate in discernment. Discernment is the ability to distinguish good spirits from evil spirits. Discernment is how we identify if our desires are healthy or an allure to the spirit of the tempter. Discernment is a spiritual function similar to the sense of smell of our physical nostrils. Just as we warm up to those things that are nicely scented and move away from foul odors, discernment is how we distinguish good and evil spirits. A typical feature of our nostrils is how when we experience the infirmity of 'cold' and temporarily lose our sharp sense of smell. In a more serious case of loss of the sense of smell, it is a medical condition known as anosmia.

The Altar of sacrifice is the place where our discernment is healed. The animal sacrifice offered sends up a scent to heaven which when accepted, changes the scent of the one who offered the sacrifice. This is what happened when Noah came out of the ark after the flood: "And Noah builded an altar unto the LORD; and took of every clean beast, and of every clean fowl, and offered burnt offerings on the altar. And the LORD smelled a sweet savour; and the LORD said in his heart, I will not again curse the ground any more for man's sake; for the imagination of man's heart is evil from his youth; neither will I again smite any more everything living, as I have done" Genesis 8:20&21. As a result of Noah's sacrifice, God changed His disposition toward mankind. The scent of the offering becomes the new scent of the one who offered the sacrifice. When we experience forgiveness at the cross, we are delivered from inhibitions, healed of our infirmities and our discernment is restored.

- ### A Path of Redemption

In this dispensation of the New Testament, the blood of Jesus lays out the path of redemption for every individual believer. "But ye are come unto mount Sion, and unto the city of the living God, the heavenly Jerusalem, and to an innumerable company of angels, To the general assembly and church of the firstborn, which are written in heaven, and to God the Judge of all, and to the spirits of just men made perfect, And to Jesus the mediator of the new covenant, and to the blood of sprinkling, that speaketh better things than that of Abel" Hebrews 12:22-24.

One of the blessings of our convocation as believers is the access to the blood of Jesus which is sprinkled upon us supernaturally. When we gather together in His name, we have corporate fellowship with His blood and we are cleansed from sin, healed and delivered. The word of His grace lays burdens upon our hearts in regards to the specific ways that we have to make peace with people who we may have hurt or those who are hurting because of our actions. In whatever way we feel the need to make peace with others is evidence of the voice of the blood of Jesus at work in our hearts. If we discount the convictions of the voice of the blood of Jesus in our lives and disregard it as our minds playing tricks on us, then we fail to leverage the power to block the activities of the spirits of vengeance. As we read earlier, the blood of Abel cries out for vengeance against Cain who murdered him.

There are certain challenges we encounter which are as a result of complex ancestral or generational fallouts. It is therefore important that we do not argue with the Holy Spirit, in regards to unusual assignments that we may not consider as being profitable to us. The voice of the blood may come as divine assignments that we receive by revelation, and may be linked to our path of redemption from certain acts of transgression, trespass or iniquity that inhibit us.

- **Harnessing Human Capital**

Human Capital is the value of the skills, knowledge, and experience possessed by those in a community or organization. You look around and observe certain communities that have been poor and remain poor for decades. Most often those people in such communities may even consider themselves cursed and their mantra may be: "nothing good ever happens here."

There are also communities that were faced with abject poverty and no prospects for development until they started to rally around a vision, harness their potentials and resources to lay the infrastructure of that community. Once the basics of a community are established, individuals within that community can pursue their dreams on that platform.

There are several things that we can achieve as individuals if we harness our personal potentials to deploy our ideas and vision. Assuming we have a great treasure of financial and material resources, we can afford to pay others to help us achieve our objectives. This is how some of the rich people in society have worked their way into success.

However, if we lack the resources to employ the services of those with the potentials to help us achieve our objectives, then we have to build a community that harnesses human capital. Ultimately, the survival and prosperity of any community or organization hinges strongly on how well human capital is harnessed. There is a trend today of discounting human capital in the corporate world that is troubling. In many instances, when there is a drop in the profits of an organization, the first culprits are the human capital. Masses of people are laid off just for the accounting records to look great in the sight of shareholders. As much as the economics of laying people off may be the quickest way to maintain high levels of profit, the overall economic impact to entire communities is often very negative. Failure to harness human capital to resolve economic challenges is a main factor responsible for how the world has remained on the edge of economic downturns and the alarming rate of poverty.

Economic stability and prosperity of people are all hinged on maintaining a balance in an economic environment. The core philosophy of an economic environment is that goods and services are produced for people by people. In an ideal scenario, as long as people remain alive in an economic environment, there should be a need for the goods and services they offer. Reality is that several other factors kick in to destabilize the economic environment such as competition, innovation and new laws. The dynamics of society makes a natural demand for us to measure up to potential factors that disrupt our economic environments.

Leadership that fails to intercede for human capital is core to the chronic poverty and instability of our world. So often we give up too soon on human capital, by failing to recognize our inherent capacity for adaptation. It is important that we recognize that within any organization are people who have the potential to foster the changes needed to measure up to the changes of that economic environment. Before we lay off people, let us first harness our adaptation potentials. It is also important that when who serve in our enterprises fallout with us but demonstrate contrition, there must be a path for redemption.

3. THE LAMP-STAND STOREHOUSE

"When that year was ended, they came unto him the second year, and said unto him, We will not hide it from my lord, how that our money is spent; my lord also hath our herds of cattle; there is not ought left in the sight of my lord, but our bodies, and our lands: Wherefore shall we die before thine eyes, both we and our land? buy us and our land for bread, and we and our land will be servants unto Pharaoh: and give us seed, that we may live, and not die, that the land be not desolate" Genesis 47:16-19.

As the famine continued unabated, the Egyptians exhausted all their money and cattle for sustenance. The Egyptians came to Joseph with an offer of their lives and lands in exchange for food. Joseph accepted their offer. At this point, there is a sense of desperation with the Egyptians. They relinquished their lives to the Pharaoh in order to have the means of sustenance. The Egyptians offer of their lives, correlates with the Lamp-stand Storehouse that Joseph had built. The Lamp-stand in the Tabernacle of Moses was seven-branched. Each branch produced a flame of light by drawing oil from a common receptacle. The Lamp was significant of the spirit of man: "The spirit of man is the candle of the LORD, searching all the inward parts of the belly" Proverbs 20:27. The oil that fueled the lamp-stand was significant of the anointing: "But ye have an unction from the Holy One, and ye know all things" 1 John 2:20.

The spiritual realm is like a very dark room where we can only access through the anointing upon our lives. Those who practice occult attempt to make penetrations into the spiritual realm illegally and so God commanded the Israelites to kill them: "Thou shalt not suffer a witch to live" Exodus 22:18. The right way to access the spiritual realm is to kindle our Lamp-stand through prayer. "Pray without ceasing. In every thing give thanks: for this is the will of God in Christ Jesus concerning you. Quench not the Spirit" 1 Thessalonians 5:17-19.

Prayer is our communication with God. It is the legitimate way to access the spiritual realm. God answers our prayers by revelations of the light of our seven-branched lamp-stand. Some of our dreams and visions are ways by which God answers our thoughts and prayers.

- **Dreams and Visions**

Dreams are revelations that we receive when asleep, while visions are revelations that we receive while awake or half-conscious. The famous story of King Nebuchadnezzar's dream in the book of Daniel throws light into the subject of dream revelations.

"And in the second year of the reign of Nebuchadnezzar Nebuchadnezzar dreamed dreams, wherewith his spirit was troubled, and his sleep brake from him. Then the king commanded to call the magicians, and the astrologers, and the sorcerers, and the Chaldeans, for to shew the king his dreams. So they came and stood before the king. And the king said unto them, I have dreamed a dream, and my spirit was troubled to know the dream...The king answered and said to Daniel, whose name was Belteshazzar, Art thou able to make known unto me the dream which I have seen, and the interpretation thereof? Daniel answered in the presence of the king, and said, The secret which the king hath demanded cannot the wise men, the astrologers, the magicians, the soothsayers, shew unto the king; But there is a God in heaven that revealeth secrets, and maketh known to the king Nebuchadnezzar what shall be in the latter days. Thy dream, and the visions of thy head upon thy bed, are these; As for thee, O king, thy thoughts came into thy mind upon thy bed, what should come to pass hereafter: and he that revealeth secrets maketh known to thee what shall come to pass. But as for me, this secret is not revealed to me for any wisdom that I have more than any living, but for their sakes that shall make known the interpretation to the king, and that thou mightest know the thoughts of thy heart" Daniel 2:1-3, 26-30.

First of all it is important to establish the premise that not all dreams are necessarily a revelation from God. We may have a dream as a result of several factors such as our emotional disposition, fears or perhaps a movie we watched and so on. In this story, King Nebuchadnezzar wakes up from the dream extremely troubled. It is the evidence of conviction that comes with a divine encounter. This is the same scenario that accompanies Pharaoh's dream of seven years of abundance followed by seven years of famine. Both kings woke up from their dreams with a strong sense of conviction. They knew it was a divine encounter and felt the essence of not ignoring the revelation. King Nebuchadnezzar commanded the wise men in Babylon to be executed if they failed to communicate the revelation of his dream, while the Pharaoh of Egypt released Joseph from prison to interpret his dream. These were extreme measures that underscored the efficacy of their convictions.

Daniel tells King Nebuchadnezzar that his dream was God's answer to his thoughts of the future: "As for thee, O king, thy thoughts came into thy mind upon thy bed, what should come to pass hereafter: and he that revealeth secrets maketh known to thee what shall come to pass." The dream came with such a strong conviction because it was a revelation from God. At the time Nebuchadnezzar's Babylonian kingdom was the superpower of the world. The dream unveiled his kingdom as gold, which would be followed by subsequently inferior kingdoms of silver, brass and iron mixed with clay. Ultimately a stone that signified God's kingdom would crush all these eras of worldly kingdoms.

The revelation of Nebuchadnezzar was a legitimate answer of God to the king of most of the known world at that time. The anointing of the Holy Spirit in us, gives us access to all information that are essential to our calling. The anointing furnishes us with the wisdom of God in all areas where we have been divinely assigned in life. The engineer, lawyer, fashion designer, pastor as well as everyone who is called into a vocation would always have access to the wisdom of God in that vocation. The key to such wisdom is prayer.

"If any of you lack wisdom, let him ask of God, that giveth to all men liberally, and upbraideth not; and it shall be given him. But let him ask in faith, nothing wavering. For he that wavereth is like a wave of the sea driven with the wind and tossed. For let not that man think that he shall receive any thing of the Lord. A double minded man is unstable in all his ways" James 1:5-8. Wisdom is available to all who ask God. The only requirement is faith. Faith is the key to receive what we seek from God. Doubt neutralizes our faith and robs us of the focus by which the mind becomes open to the revelations of wisdom. To further underscore God's liberality with wisdom, Jesus taught His disciples: "Ask and it will be given to you; seek and you will find; knock and the door will be opened to you. For everyone who asks receives; the one who seeks finds; and to the one who knocks, the door will be opened" Matthew 7:7&8. As simple as this three letter word 'ask' is, it is yet the most difficult thing for mankind to do in relation to God. There are so many books, expensive experiments, expeditions and documentary films with so much assumption that could be resolved if we would ask God with the right attitude of faith. I wonder how else it could have been stated in the scriptures to make it easy for mankind to accept the access path for wisdom that God is so willing to divulge.

Several years ago a business woman who had received a huge loan for her imports came to see me. Time was not in her favor and she was just about to default on her loan payments which could ruin her business credibility with the bank. I requested that she take me on a tour of her establishment and so we visited her retail and warehouse locations which were all filled with assorted products she had imported.

Her capital was tied up because sales were very slow regardless of all contemporary marketing strategies she had applied. My solution to her was simple. I told her to pray and ask God for which particular product would give her a breakthrough. The following day she came back to see me to tell me a dream she had after praying to God to seek wisdom. God revealed a particular product as standing out at the warehouse. She imported large quantities of this product and the sales were phenomenal. Her breakthrough came because she asked for wisdom from God and she got it.

- **Barrenness**

Any area of life where we are unable to produce the desired results is a condition of barrenness. Other words associated with barrenness include: unfruitfulness, lack, poverty, emotional frustration, divorce and so on. All these words indicate that barrenness could be spiritual, emotional, physical or financial.

The design of the lamp-stand of the tabernacle of Moses was seven-branched with each branch designed with almond-shaped knobs to depict fruitfulness. This tells us that the lamp-stand is where we overcome every form of barrenness. The anointing of the Holy Spirit facilitates fruitfulness in every area of our lives. We are three-dimensional human beings: we are spirit; we have a soul and live in a body. Three of the trees in the Garden of Eden where God placed

Adam and Eve were designed to furnish him to flourish spiritually, emotionally and financially. These were the tree of life, the tree pleasant to sight and the tree good for food respectively. The anointing of the Holy Spirit is the oil from these trees that equip us to be fruitful spiritually, emotionally and financially. "For this very reason, make every effort to add to your faith goodness; and to goodness, knowledge; and to knowledge, self-control; and to self-control, perseverance; and to perseverance, godliness; and to godliness, mutual affection; and to mutual affection, love. For if you possess these qualities in increasing measure, they will keep you from being ineffective and unproductive in your knowledge of our Lord Jesus Christ" 2 Peter 2:5-8.

Notice that in this scripture, we are admonished to 'add' the fruits of the Spirit to our 'faith.' Such fruits of the Spirit include goodness, knowledge, self-control, perseverance, godliness, mutual affection and love. Our faith is the most exciting aspect of our relationship with God because we have great promises from God which makes us hopeful for a great future. However most of us fall short of the fruits of the spirit which are fundamental to experiencing the manifestation of the promises of God.

The Apostle Peter says: "if you possess these qualities in increasing measure, they will keep you from being ineffective and unproductive in your knowledge of our Lord Jesus Christ." The words, 'ineffective and unproductive' mean barrenness. In other words the apostle is saying that without adding the fruits of the Spirit to our faith, we become barren. The Holy Spirit does not only convey to us promises of God but also the process for inheriting these promises. The anointing furnishes us with step-by-step guidance that altogether constitutes the wisdom of God.

- ## Land, Seed and Bread

To disrupt a condition of barrenness, we have to engage the appropriate divine concept. The word 'concept' is another way of expressing the word 'conceive' or become pregnant. Three core elements of a pregnancy are: Womb, Sperm and Egg. Similarly any divine concept that tends to fruitfulness must entail the elements of land, seed and bread. "Then God said, "Let the land produce vegetation: seed-bearing plants and trees on the land that bear fruit with seed in it, according to their various kinds" And it was so" Genesis 1:11.

LAND: Land is significant of the attitude of man's heart towards divine revelation. Attitude is the logos dimension of any concept that becomes fruitful. In the parable of the sower, Jesus taught about the relationship of the attitudes of the heart with fruitfulness. "Now the parable is this: The seed is the word of God. Those by the way side are they that hear; then cometh the devil, and taketh away the word out of their hearts, lest they should believe and be saved. They on the rock are they, which, when they hear, receive the word with joy; and these have no root, which for a while believe, and in time of temptation fall away. And that which fell among thorns are they, which, when they have heard, go forth, and are choked with cares and riches and pleasures of this life, and bring no fruit to perfection. But that on the good ground are they, which in an honest and good heart, having heard the word, keep it, and bring forth fruit with patience" Luke 8:11-15.

Four kinds of heart are described in this scripture: wayside heart, rocky heart, thorny heart and good heart. The wayside heart hears God's word but does not believe it so cannot retain the knowledge. The rocky heart believes God's word but does not have understanding so cannot withstand temptation. The thorny heart believes and understands God's word but lacks focus and so gets distracted and derailed after a while. The good heart is the attitude that believes God's word, understands it, is focused and bears fruit with patience.

Belief, understand, focus and patience are the four attitudes that altogether makes us fruitful. In the same way a farmer prepares the soil before seeds are sown, these attitudes must be cultivated in the heart so that we become fruitful in every area of our lives. The teaching of God's logos-word, gives us the framework of mind to receive and thrive rhema-word.

SEED: Seed in the parable of Jesus was significant of God's rhema-word. Seed is the divine revelation of the primary process of any vocation or product. In business we commonly refer to this as the investment stage. "Give ye ear, and hear my voice; hearken, and hear my speech. Doth the plowman plow all day to sow? doth he open and break the clods of his ground? When he hath made plain the face thereof, doth he not cast abroad the fitches, and scatter the cummin, and cast in the principal wheat and the appointed barley and the rie in their place? For his God doth instruct him to discretion, and doth teach him" Isaiah 28:23-26.

God teaches the farmer the process of seed for any particular crop. It is the function of the anointing that furnishes every called professional with the revelation of the preliminary steps of their endeavor. Access to the seed process for advancing the vocation of our calling should never come as a challenge.

BREAD: This is the harvest process. The final stage of a productive process is the bread-harvest. The bread-harvest is also rhema inspired. In the parable of the sower, Jesus mentions various levels of harvest that is thirtyfold, sixtyfold and hundredfold. The level of harvest is incumbent upon the methods employed. "For the fitches are not threshed with a threshing instrument, neither is a cart wheel turned about upon the cummin; but the fitches are beaten out with a staff, and the cummin with a rod. Bread corn is bruised; because he will not ever be threshing it, nor break it with the wheel of his cart, nor bruise it with his horsemen. This also cometh forth from the LORD of hosts, which is wonderful in counsel, and excellent in working" Isaiah 28:27-29.

God furnishes us with wonderful counsel for an excellent harvest. If we ignore God's willingness to furnish us with the harvest process, then we rob ourselves of the potential for a maximum harvest.

- **Thoughts**

The thought or intellect is a function of the mind where we rationalize information. This is where we make sense of information we have access to. As believers we have access to knowledge of scriptural truths also known as the logos-word, we also have the opportunity for divine insights also known as the rhema-word as well as access to facts. Wisdom is that dimension of revelation that incorporates logos-word knowledge, rhema-word insights as well as relevant factual information. The process of harnessing logos-word knowledge, rhema-word insights and relevant facts to bear on a mission qualifies as an intellectual thought.

As we saw earlier, God answered King Nebuchadnezzar's thoughts with a dream. When our thoughts are pure and focused on our calling and vocation, God answers us through a function of the anointing. The Apostle Paul encourages us in Philippians 4:8: "Finally, brethren, whatsoever things are true, whatsoever things are honest, whatsoever things are just, whatsoever things are pure, whatsoever things are lovely, whatsoever things are of good report; if there be any virtue, and if there be any praise, think on these things."

It is from the scriptures that we know things that are true, honest, just, pure, lovely, good report, virtue and praise. Our thoughts must always be hinged on the desire to fulfill the divine values we learn from scriptures. Next our thoughts must be focused on executing the divine revelation that points to our assignment or mission. Finally our thoughts would be lacking unless we incorporate research of the relevant facts of that assignment or mission. When all three factors of wisdom are in alignment, the stage is set for God to unveil the next level of wisdom which is what we do not yet know. God inserts himself into our mission with unusual wisdom that represents the future of what we are endeavoring to achieve.

- **Reverse Engineering**

During the Second World War, the Germans under Hitler used an enigma machine to transmit coded messages to the soldiers on the frontline of the battle. As a result, the British and allied forces could not predict the moves of the Germans who often launched surprise attacks successfully. A brilliant British mathematician by name Alan Turing was able to decode the messages of the enigma machine through the process of reverse engineering. Reverse engineering involves dismantling a product to figure out how it was put together to function. This development contributed in accelerating the ability of the Allies to overcome Nazi Germany. It is estimated that the work of Alan Turing contributed immensely to ending the Second World War two years earlier.

The wisdom of any objective or product is the sum of micro-steps by which it functions. Most things that God would have us achieve or produce may already have similar models available. Most often God wants to take us to the next level of that model so it is important that we acquaint ourselves with the existing model. The process by which we familiarize with how an existing model functions is what is known as reverse engineering.

Reverse engineering is also the process by which we can interpret a divine revelation of wisdom and write out the micro-process for accomplishing it. "Remember the former things, those of long ago; I am God, and there is no other; I am God, and there is none like me. I make known the end from the beginning, from ancient times, what is still to come. I say, 'My purpose will stand, and I will do all that I please" Isaiah 46:9&10.

God reveals wisdom in a three-dimension way that is the past, present and future. Knowledge is the revelation of the past; Understanding is the revelation of the present while Wisdom is the revelation of the future. The revelation of wisdom thrives upon the fundamentals of knowledge and understanding. God revealed the existing models of any process or product to previous generations. Existing models are the legacy of the present generation to inherit. If we ignore the wisdom of an existing model, all our efforts to create would amount to 'reinventing the wheel.'

"And they shall build the old wastes, they shall raise up the former desolations, and they shall repair the waste cities, the desolations of many generations" Isaiah 61:4. The reason God unveils wisdom is to take a generation of people to the next level, so He unveils a vision of what is not yet invented. However to accomplish a new thing, we must be well acquainted with the past and present. When the wisdom of God is injected into an existing model, it becomes more efficient and achieves greater results.

4. TABLE OF SHOWBREAD STOREHOUSE

"And Joseph bought all the land of Egypt for Pharaoh; for the Egyptians sold every man his field, because the famine prevailed over them: so the land became Pharaoh's. And as for the people, he removed them to cities from one end of the borders of Egypt even to the other end thereof. Only the land of the priests bought he not; for the priests had a portion assigned them of Pharaoh, and did eat their portion which Pharaoh gave them: wherefore they sold not their lands" Genesis 47:20-22.

Land was the last valuable asset of the Egyptians and they offered it to Joseph for their sustenance. This deal of exchange of land for food gave Joseph a complete takeover of the wealth of the Egyptians. With the exception of the priests, Joseph now had the liberty of reassigning the Egyptians to live wherever he deemed fit. From food cultivation, mineral resource mining, timber logging to fishing, land holds the potential treasures of all material wealth. Joseph's acquisition of the land extended the authority of the Pharaoh to an inconceivable extent. Absolute ownership of the land of Egypt resulted in unhinged royalty for the Pharaoh of Egypt.

The Table of Showbread in the tabernacle of Moses was constructed with acacia wood and overlaid with gold. The top of the table was molded as the design of the crown of a king. This table was significant of royalty. Twelve loaves of bread were placed on this table to signify divine providence for the twelve tribes of Israel. The bread was replaced on a weekly basis that is significant of the weekly message of God to the congregation of His people. Usually the head of a local Church would wait on God and bring a message for the main weekly gathering of the Church. This word is God's providence for his people. It is usually an inspiring instruction that is a mix of rhema-word and logos-word.

The inspiring instruction from the table of showbread is a word of royalty. It equips the believer with the ability to reign in a space of legitimate jurisdiction. Everyone has a space where they must exercise authority. A father and mother have authority over their immediate family. An employee and supervisor have authority over their employees. A governor or mayor has authority over their constituency. A minister has divine authority over their congregants. In any sphere of life where we are legitimately placed in charge of people or territory, we have a form of royal authority.

- **Dress it and Keep it**

God's word to us from the pulpit empowers us to develop and defend our royal jurisdictions. "And the LORD God took the man, and put him into the garden of Eden to dress it and to keep it" Genesis 2:15. The Garden of Eden was Adam and Eve's jurisdiction of royal authority until they fell from grace. They were driven out of the Garden of Eden to live in a hostile environment where they had to fight for survival. We thank God for the blessing of restoration in Christ Jesus.

Our divine authority to reign prosperously over our territorial jurisdiction is enshrined in the rhema-logos word. It encapsulates God's wisdom and the power to defend our space. Most often our attitude is to only draw inspiration from the message but fail to apply the wisdom and power of the word during the week. Wherever we are blessed with royal jurisdiction, our mandate is to dress and keep. To 'dress our garden' gives the sense of a farmer cultivating the field, a shepherd tending the sheep or a blacksmith forging weapons. It is important that we leverage the wisdom of the rhema-logos word to bear on the practice of our vocation, leadership of family and ministry in order to flourish in these endeavors.

Any opposition we encounter while applying divine wisdom is an attempt of the enemy to encroach on our space. For this reason we must have a mindset of 'keeping the garden.' Within the rhema-logos that come from the pulpit is the revelation strategy to outwit the enemy. It is important that we never throw our hands up in despair because we have the power of God incorporated in the rhema-logos word to defend our space at all times. As spiritual, family and occupational leaders we must spend more time with the rhema-logos word that comes from the pulpit in order to draw the full wisdom and power of God to both dress and keep our space.

- **Royalty Coordinates**

The South, North, East and West are the natural geographic coordinates for any territory. How a king grasps these four coordinates determines to a large extent how prosperous he can become.

SOUTH: A cardinal principle of royalty is the essence of knowledge. A king must have surveyors who map out the land and demarcate its borders and regions. All regions must be identified with their potential resources outlined. With such knowledge it is possible to craft laws to protect these resources and the overall territory.

NORTH: A king must not only become aware of, but have a deep grasp of the material resources and potentials embedded within his geographical and cosmic territory. For instance, if there is gold in the land, it is important to understand its total utility as well as how it is mined and sold. A diligent king will also be interested in the spiritual significance of the resource and why it is uniquely available as a blessing in his space.

EAST: A king must develop a blueprint for harnessing the potentials within his space. To do this, the king assembles teams of experts who will be mandated to do diligent research of the identified resources, how they can be properly harnessed and deployed to bring benefits to the kingdom. It is commonly said that 'failure to plan is a plan to fail.'

WEST: The goals enshrined in the blueprint, becomes the road map for developing and advancing the king's domain. Government Commissions, Departments and Enterprises are established to manage specific aspects of the plan. Furthermore, a king develops covenant relationships by which he deploys the resources in the land to achieve his goals.

• Covenant Relationships

We have just learnt about the four ways by which kings administer their territory successfully. The first way is to have their royal space properly demarcated. The second way is they must have a good grasp of all potentials and resources within their territory. Thirdly, they must have a versatile plan to harness these resources. Finally they must develop relationships with their constituents and with other kings with whom they can develop and exchange their resources. Let us take a deeper look into the fourth way of royal administration that is covenant relationships.

"And Isaac's servants digged in the valley, and found there a well of springing water. And the herdmen of Gerar did strive with Isaac's herdmen, saying, The water is ours: and he called the name of the well Esek; because they strove with him. And they digged another well, and strove for that also: and he called the name of it Sitnah. And he removed from thence, and digged another well; and for that they strove not: and he called the name of it Rehoboth; and he said, For now the LORD hath made room for us, and we shall be fruitful in the land" Genesis 26:19-22.

The backdrop to the scripture above was a condition of famine during the life of Isaac the son of Abraham. During the lifetime of Abraham he had dug four wells but the Philistines seized these wells when he died and covered them with earth. In the face of the famine, Isaac resolved in his heart to relocate to

Egypt in order to survive. However, before he made this move, God visited him and dissuaded him from relocating to Egypt. Isaac remained in the land of Gerar and began to revive the four wells of his father Abraham.

When he revived the first well, the Philistines resisted him and he called the name Esek. The second well he revived was also challenged by the Philistines and he called it Sitnah. The third well he dug was never challenged so he named it Rehoboth. From this point onwards Isaac begun to flourish. He was so fruitful that the Philistines who had opposed him in every way possible noticed his unusual phenomenal success in the time of famine.

"And he went up from thence to Beersheba. And the LORD appeared unto him the same night, and said, I am the God of Abraham thy father: fear not, for I am with thee, and will bless thee, and multiply thy seed for my servant Abraham's sake. And he builded an altar there, and called upon the name of the LORD, and pitched his tent there: and there Isaac's servants digged a well. Then Abimelech went to him from Gerar, and Ahuzzath one of his friends, and Phichol the chief captain of his army. And Isaac said unto them, Wherefore come ye to me, seeing ye hate me, and have sent me away from you? And they said, We saw certainly that the LORD was with thee: and we said, Let there be now an oath betwixt us, even betwixt us and thee, and let us make a covenant with thee; That thou wilt do us no hurt, as we have not touched thee, and as we have done unto thee nothing but good, and have sent thee away in peace: thou art now the blessed of the LORD. And he made them a feast, and they did eat and drink. And they rose up betimes in the morning, and sware one to another: and Isaac sent them away, and they departed from him in peace. And it came to pass the same day, that Isaac's servants came, and told him concerning the well which they had digged, and said unto him, We have found water. And he called it Shebah: therefore the name of the city is Beersheba unto this day" Genesis 26:23-33.

There are many objectives that we can accomplish in life if only we have the resources to afford them. However, there are some objectives which we can only accomplish within the framework of covenant relationships. Abimelech the Philistine king had resisted Isaac in every way possible and yet Isaac was successful in every way imaginable. There is a common saying: "If you cannot beat them, you join them", so King Abimelech came knocking on Isaac's door to seek a covenant relationship.

Covenant relationships prevent kings from warring against each other so they can peacefully coexist. This way they trade with one another and even collaborate on ventures of mutual interest. As individuals, we are potentially kings and are surrounded by people in every sphere of life who are also kings. It is important that we identify those with whom we must establish covenant relationships of mutual benefit.

"And Hiram king of Tyre sent messengers to David, and cedar trees, and carpenters, and masons: and they built David an house. And David perceived that the LORD had established him king over Israel, and that he had exalted his kingdom for his people Israel's sake" 2 Samuel 5:11&12. The scriptures tell us that when King Saul the first monarch in Israel died, the Israelites anointed David to become king of Israel. Very early in his reign, King David received an entourage from a heathen king of Tyre. They brought King David building materials and a workforce of skilled artisans to build him a palace. King David was surprised at this gesture but also sees the hand of God in all of these. First of all, God wanted to indicate to King David that the world of kings around him acknowledged his anointed royalty. Secondly, God wanted King David to know that King Hiram was a potential for a covenant relationship.

- **The Will**

You will notice that the first three storehouses of Joseph had a relationship with the configuration of the human mind. The Brazen Laver Storehouse is the place of 'Conscience'; the Altar of Sacrifice Storehouse is the place of 'Emotion'; while the Lampstand Storehouse is the place of our 'Thoughts.' In the same token, the Table of Showbread Storehouse is the place of the 'Will.' The Will is the ultimate of all mental process where we initiate the move to carry out our resolve.

Our covenant relationships play an integral role in how we make decisions that determine our pursuits. Covenant relationships establish boundaries for whatever we do. We exercise our will first of all to draw from the benefits of covenant relationships and to preserve these relationships. This way, we receive a constant flow of the resources we need to continue our pursuits unhindered.

The human will feeds upon the virtue of loyalty to make decisions that prevent unnecessary conflicts. Without loyalty to a covenant relationship, peaceful coexistence cannot be guaranteed. Furthermore, it is crucial that we respect the limitations of a covenant relationship and avoid crossing boundaries. For instance, try not to prematurely mix a business relationship with family as much as possible. Let relationships grow from one level to another on a natural pace and not artificially.

The Church is a natural support system for Christians which has not being properly harnessed to undergird our individual pursuits of destiny. The message of loyalty has been mostly directed toward our commitment to Christ and the Church but not toward one another as believers. I believe Christians would make greater progress in their pursuit of divine destiny if only we become more aware of the benefits of loyalty to our intra-Christian relationships. Everyone within a network of support must apply themselves to unwavering commitment to one another so they can thrive and achieve their individual aspirations as well as corporate prosperity.

- **Royalty Foundations**

Throughout the history of humanity we observe from the scriptures that God has an intention to establish us in royalty. Theologians have identified seven major covenants in the bible, and insight into these covenant relationships clearly unveil God's desire for man to function as royals.

ADAM: Destiny and Carnality

When God created Adam, he was placed in the Garden of Eden where God planted four kinds of trees. The tree pleasant to the sight, the tree good for food and the tree of life were significant of man's emotional, financial and spiritual destiny so God allowed Adam access to them. However, the tree of the knowledge of good and evil was significant of the carnal man and so God instructed Adam not to eat of it. Adam started out to work in the naming of animals that were in the garden. A name is the nature and character of an object or person. Adam essentially gave function and purpose to all the animals in the garden. The serpent was given a name 'nakash' which means 'diviner' or one who hears from the spirit. This name became an access way for the devil to enter the garden and pervert God's intentions for man. As we all know, this is how the earth became cursed and much misery was introduced into our humanity. The big picture here is that God created man with legislative power to give function and purpose to all creation. If we yield to divine inspiration in fulfilling this function, we empower creation to function as God intended and effectively deny the enemy access to our garden of royalty.

NOAH: Creation and Judgment

The people in Noah's day were very evil and so God destroyed them by a flood. Noah and his family were saved from this destruction by the ark which God led him to build. After the flood, Noah offered sacrifices for which reason God made a covenant never to destroy the earth again with flood waters. God established the framework for seasonal cycles such as day and night, winter and summer, cold and heat as well as seedtime and harvest time. Not long after this covenant was established, the people of that era felt that they could not trust God to keep that covenant so they decided to build a tower to protect them against a flood from God. When God saw their intentions, He confused their language so they could not understand one another and stopped the project. Throughout history, it is noteworthy that whenever people have attempted to build anything that resembles the tower of Babel, such intentions ultimately comes under divine judgment and never endures. The lesson here is that God desires to work with humanity through the framework of seasons by which we can build an ark that preserves us in time of judgment.

ABRAHAM: Blessings and Curses

God called Abraham to leave his country and people for a new heritage. By this heritage, Abraham would become the root of blessings. At this point however, Abraham and his wife Sarah had no child and God promised them a child. After a long time had passed, Abraham and Sarah decided to succumb to the culture of that time where a maid could be made to have children for her mistress. Hagar the maid of Sarah gives birth to Ishmael which is contrary to God's plan for Abraham. Later when Sarah has a son for Abraham there is rivalry between Sarah and Hagar for which reason Hagar and her son Ishmael are evicted from Abraham's household. Hagar's son Ishmael is born out of customary practice while Sarah's son Isaac was born as a fulfillment of God's promise to Abraham. Ishmael represents the flesh while Isaac represents the Spirit. All blessings from God are rooted in Abraham. "Christ hath redeemed us from the curse of the law, being made a curse for us: for it is written, Cursed is every one that hangeth on a tree: That the blessing of Abraham might come on the Gentiles through Jesus Christ; that we might receive the promise of the Spirit through faith" Galatians 3:13&14. The lesson in Abraham is that all blessings are tied up in the promises of the Spirit.

Royalty requires that in whatever area of life we desire blessings, we must seek to align with a promise of the Spirit.

MOSES: Lawful and Unlawful

When Moses finally secures the release of the Israelites from the enslavement in Egypt, God leads them through the wilderness to establish them as a nation. Moses is given approximately six hundred laws of which half are instructions to fulfill, while the other half are instructions to refrain from certain acts. Laws are the fundamentals of the government of a nation. At some point in their journey in the wilderness, the Israelites needed water and Moses was given an instruction from God to speak to a rock to provide water supernaturally. Moses himself violates this divine instruction and is denied access to the Promised Land. "And Moses lifted up his hand, and with his rod he smote the rock twice: and the water came out abundantly, and the congregation drank, and their beasts also. And the LORD spake unto Moses and Aaron, Because ye believed me not, to sanctify me in the eyes of the children of Israel, therefore ye shall not bring this congregation into the land which I have given them" Numbers 20:11&12. Obedience to divine instructions is fundamental to any government of royalty.

PALESTINE: Dominion and Disenfranchisement

The Land of Palestine is a specific territory that God promised to Abraham for an inheritance. Moses leads the Israelites from Egypt with this Promised Land as their destination. God established the framework for keeping this territory. A key instruction is to observe the seventh year land rest Sabbaths. When the Israelites fail to observe the seventh year land rest Sabbaths and accumulate seventy years of debt to the land, they are evicted from the land and sent into exile in Babylon. The key lesson of the Palestine covenant is that God assigns every king with a specific domain as their territory and there are fundamental rules by which such a domain is maintained.

DAVID: Mercy and Wickedness

When Saul is rejected as king of Israel, God instructs the prophet Samuel to anoint David who is from the tribe of Judah as a replacement. King David starts out as a prosperous ruler until one day he spots Bathsheba the wife of Urriah a soldier at war having a shower. The king commits adultery with Bathsheba and arranges for her husband Urriah to be placed at the front lines of the battle where he dies. God is displeased with King David and sends Nathan the prophet to rebuke him. "And Nathan said to David, Thou art the man. Thus saith the LORD God of Israel, I anointed thee king over Israel, and I delivered thee out of the hand of Saul; And I gave thee thy master's house, and thy master's wives into thy bosom, and gave thee the house of Israel and of Judah; and if that had been too little, I would moreover have given unto thee such and such things. Wherefore hast thou despised the commandment of the LORD, to do evil in his sight? thou hast killed Uriah the Hittite with the sword, and hast taken his wife to be thy wife, and hast slain him with the sword of the children of Ammon. Now therefore the sword shall never depart from thine house; because thou hast despised me, and hast taken the wife of Uriah the Hittite to be thy wife. Thus saith the LORD, Behold, I will raise up evil against thee out of thine own house, and I will take thy wives before thine eyes, and give them unto thy neighbour, and he shall lie with thy wives in the sight of this sun" 2 Samuel 12:7-11.

The main point of Nathan's discourse is that King David committed acts of wickedness against Urriah which was absolutely unnecessary. He could have simply asked God for what he desired as a king and God would have furnished him in a legitimate way. From this point onwards, the peaceful reign of King David was marred with rebellions that upset his throne. "It is an abomination to kings to commit wickedness: for the throne is established by righteousness" Proverbs 16:12. The wickedness of a king upsets his throne. True royalty thrives on the wings of merciful acts. Peasants who want to enjoy the preserve of royals act covetously to steal from people.

NEW COVENANT: Grace and Disfavor

Salvation through Jesus Christ is how we enter into a new covenant with God. The blood of animal sacrifices is no longer required to ratify a covenant with God. Rather it is our salvation through Jesus Christ that ushers us into the New Covenant. The New Covenant hinges on the blood that Jesus Christ shed for us on the cross of Calvary. This New Covenant ushers us into the dispensation of grace. Grace means that we do not have to offer up animal sacrifices for our sins. If we repent and confess our sins, the blood of Jesus Christ cleanses us from all unrighteousness. Grace also gives us access to the power of God to overcome sin in our lives. During His life here on earth, our Lord Jesus Christ taught us how to operate in royalty through the principles of the kingdom. Ultimately as we yield ourselves to apply the gospel of the kingdom in our ways, we shall experience the fullness and blessings of royalty in the kingdom of Christ.

- **Hexagon Quadrilateral**

Though taking over a territory is an important task for anyone who wants to run an enterprise, government, ministry, institution or any significant endeavor, the most critical task is the ability to maintain and advance the territory after the conquest. For instance, getting hired for the job of CEO of a huge corporation is not as difficult as spurring and sustaining its growth after assuming office.

When the Israelites were at the threshold of the Promised Land, Moses selected the leaders of the twelve tribes of Israel to go and spy out the land. The hexagon quadrilateral is the royal mindset by which Moses expected the tribal leaders of Israel to evaluate six benchmarks of the Promised Land. These six benchmarks were Mission, Human Resource, Corporate Resource, Productivity, Market and Finance. Constant evaluation of these six benchmarks of any domain or endeavor with a royal mindset is the core function of any leader. The success of the endeavor hinges on how effective a leader analyses these benchmarks and determines his quadrilateral mindset of goals, objectives, strategy and tactics.

GOALS or CHALLENGES: Most often people interchange the word Goal with Vision. The distinction here is that while Vision is that overall desire and extent of accomplishment for an endeavor, Goals are the core challenges that an endeavor must confront in order to become successful. The core goals of any endeavor are six-fold and they are Mission, Human Resource, Corporate Resource, Productivity, Market and Finance. These six benchmarks will pose six different sets of challenges to any endeavor and the leader must primarily seek to understand the scope of these challenges.

During the time of Moses, print technology was not available so he had to deploy the leadership of the twelve tribes as typical foot-soldier-spies to explore the Promised Land. Today while such field research is necessary in some cases to get hard facts, it is possible to obtain a lot of information today from internet search, libraries, and books as well as from trade and professional associations. A typical goal could be an industry problem either present or projected. Such industry problems could range from compliance with government regulation, consumer complains, costing, pricing, community grievances etc. You are able to quickly penetrate an industry and make a significant impact if you can identify the shortfalls and present solutions that mitigate them. The reason identifying challenges to determine goals are core to leadership is that tackling such goals gives you immediate significance and hence a demand. Wherever there is a natural demand for which you can fill the supply, a market is established and success is inevitable.

OBJECTIVES or INITIATIVES: Most often people use the words 'goals' and 'objectives' interchangeably. Technically, while a goal is associated with a challenge, an objective is usually associated with a well defined initiative. An objective is how you intend to address a goal. It is an initiative that tackles a challenge head-on. A good objective must be specific, measurable, achievable or affordable, time-sensitive. The role of leadership is to be able to initiate a well defined objective that hits the 'nail on the head.' When a good objective is accomplished it does not only address the challenge at hand, but it becomes the platform or stepping stone to achieve other goals.

STRATEGIES / RESOURCE HARNESS: Strategy is how you effectively harness your resources to attain your objective. As you will notice the process of a royal mindset started out by identifying a goal or challenge, then it was followed by an objective or initiative to address the goal. The next step of a royal mindset is the development of strategy that is, how do we harness our available resources in such a way as to achieve our objective. Most often our resources are very limited in the face of the objective. A typical story in scriptures is the Goliath versus David encounter. While Goliath is a military authority of the day, heavily armed and sophisticated, David on the other hand is young, with no military experience and only accustomed to the feeble sling and stone used in bird hunting. This contest looks like a mismatch in every way but then David has a strategy. He changes the goal of the contest from Goliath's original quest for human domination to a divine sentence against Goliath for spiritual defiance of the God of Israel. By changing the subject of the contest to divinity against humanity, David gets God to fight on his behalf. Strategy is how we leverage God's word to bear on our resources to achieve our objectives. Several miracles in the scriptures underscore why we should never underestimate our resources if only we can incorporate a divine revelation. Elisha gives a divine instruction to the indebted widow and her jar of oil is multiplied to fill many jars by which her debt is paid and her family is sustained. Jesus Christ multiplied five loaves and two fishes to feed thousands of people and yet there were twelve baskets of leftovers.

TACTICS or OPPORTUNITIES DEPLOYMENT: A tactic is how you implement a strategy. Tactic is the last aspect of the royal mindset and it entails the processes, methods and tasks by which we execute the strategy. In the story of Goliath and David, the tactic is deployed when David hurls the stone from the sling and takes down Goliath in a humiliating defeat. While the role of determining the goals, initiating objectives and developing a strategy are all functions of leadership, tactics are implemented by the human resource team and covenant partners. Tactics are the tasks assigned to those who work for you. Each task must spell out the method to be applied, the resources to be engaged as well as those who must execute the task and the time frame. Generally people shy away from difficult and highly demanding tasks so the smart way of generating the interest of people to undertake a task or collaborate with its implementation is to unveil the opportunities that come with it. The reward is the core motivation for garnering people's participation as it is commonly said: "show me the money and then we would tango" also "no finance no romance."

5. THE ALTAR OF INCENSE STOREHOUSE

"Then Joseph said unto the people, Behold, I have bought you this day and your land for Pharaoh: lo, here is seed for you, and ye shall sow the land" Genesis 47:25. Joseph has closed on an extraordinary deal in which he procures all the Egyptians and their lands for the Pharaoh. They no longer own their lives and have to live to please the Pharaoh at all times. The Pharaoh is now a god to the Egyptians and this is the fundamental basis of worship. Joseph reassigns the Egyptians to wherever he deems fit according to their potentials and gives them the appropriate seeds to be sown.

The Altar of Incense is the next progression from royalty and Joseph has effectively elevated the Pharaoh to the status of a deity. In the tabernacle of Moses, the altar of incense is the realm of divinity. Here at this altar, four specific spices which are frankincense, onycha, stacte and galbanum were burned as worship incense to God (Exodus 30:34-37).

Frankincense: This spice is a whitish substance that depicts inspired righteousness. Whenever we receive revelation to study specific scriptures or our Ministers are divinely inspired to teach us specific instruction from the scriptures, such a word that we apply to our lives send up frankincense to God.

Onycha: This spice is significant of inspired intercession. Whenever we are divinely inspired to pray specific topics or for specific people and travail in prayer in these areas, such prayer is significant of onycha.

Stacte: This spice is significant of inspired adoration. Sometimes we are inspired with a song in our hearts and may start singing or the music leader during worship is divinely inspired to start a song and we all join in singing. Such inclination to adore God by divine inspiration is significant of stacte.

Galbanum: This spice is significant of the fat of offerings. Whenever we are divinely inspired to give offerings to specific people or causes, the aroma of galbanum rises to God.

In the case of the Egyptians, Joseph provided them with seeds to sow the fields he had allocated to them. This way they will serve the Pharaoh with their lives in order to have sustenance. In the context of the New Testament believer, the Apostle Paul says in Romans 12:1&2: "I beseech you therefore, brethren, by the mercies of God, that ye present your bodies a living sacrifice, holy, acceptable unto God, which is your reasonable service. And be not conformed to this world: but be ye transformed by the renewing of your mind, that ye may prove what is that good, and acceptable, and perfect, will of God." The Altar of

Incense is that dimension where our entire lives become subject to the will of God. The four spices of incense are like divine charges to the believer. Throughout the scriptures we see various instances where God gives a specific charge to His people or leaders. The usage of the word 'charge' implies a lot both literally and significantly as the spice of incense. We charge the battery of our cell phones with power, we charge our credit cards in payments, the commander of a military force issues a charge to advance the fight against the enemy. Divine inspiration is how we receive a supernatural charge to advance beyond our human limitations into the realm of divinity.

- **Angelic Collaboration**

The Altar of Incense Storehouse is the realm of divinity. Here we collaborate with angels to accomplish divine goals. Most of the promises we receive from God in relation to our destiny are usually phenomenal. "According as his divine power hath given unto us all things that pertain unto life and godliness, through the knowledge of him that hath called us to glory and virtue: Whereby are given unto us exceeding great and precious promises: that by these ye might be partakers of the divine nature, having escaped the corruption that is in the world through lust" 2 Peter 1:3&4.

Apostle Peter describes God's promises to us as being "exceeding great and precious." We all have in us the potential to achieve tremendous greatness in accomplishment despite our mediocre beginnings and resources. This is possible because of the availability of divine power, which is how angels apply themselves to our works. Owing to the promises of God which are often beyond our own capabilities, we can partake of the divine nature through collaboration with angels. If our goals are divine, we have access to the realm of divinity. Throughout the scriptures we learn of two kinds of angels that are Cherubim and Seraphim. While Cherubim are known to carry out God's instructions, Seraphim execute man's instructions. By reassigning the Egyptians with land and seed that reflects their divine destiny, Joseph reorganizes Egypt based upon this premise of the realm of divinity. Every Egyptian is now functioning in the arena of their divine destiny and so there is a fundamental collaboration with angels. In this dimension, their humanity is infused with divinity and so greater accomplishments are possible. It is no wonder that historically, Egypt is known to have been at the forefront of the advancement of civilization in the entire world. Today many in the world of science and innovation attribute the phenomenal advancements in math and scientific knowledge to cosmic revelations from alien sources provided to selected humans who we classify as being genius. This and similar assertions only allude to what has always been enshrined in the scriptures as the realm of divinity where angels collaborate with humans who are appropriately inclined.

When Isaac Newton, Albert Einstein and other scientists harnessed their focus to bear on specific goals they received the attention of angels whom scientists describe as extraterrestrial or alien beings. Fundamentally the scripture teaches that God does not hold back wisdom from those who seek for it with a single eye. "If any of you lack wisdom, let him ask of God, that giveth to all men liberally, and upbraideth not; and it shall be given him. But let him ask in faith, nothing wavering. For he that wavereth is like a wave of the sea driven with the wind and tossed. For let not that man think that he shall receive any thing of the Lord. A double minded man is unstable in all his ways" James 1:5-8.

While it may be true that people are selected for phenomenal revelation, this selection is contingent on some basic premises that preclude any form of favoritism. First of all, the scripture says that God is liberal in how He dispenses wisdom. Secondly, whoever seeks wisdom must not doubt. This means there must be a strong sense of discipline and focus. Common to all accomplished scientists and inventors is the essence of discipline and focus. It requires deep passion for the subject and tenacity of purpose. The unwavering commitment to discover the unknown in an area is by itself a burden that is entirely divine. Anyone who harnesses the energy of deep passion and burden to a specific goal garners the attention of angels. Many Mathematicians, Scientists are known to have received accurate solutions to their mental quests by way of dream revelations. Jesus taught the principle here in Matthew 6:22: "The light of the body is the eye: if therefore thine eye be single, thy whole body shall be full of light." It is important that we accept the scriptural premise that we all have access to angelic revelation and collaboration. Essentially if we would reposition ourselves in our divine calling and harness the deep passion and burden of our divine assignment into a single eye, such focus will connect us to mysteries that become the basis for phenomenal creativity.

- **Divine Alignment**

There is so much inherent potential within every human being which unfortunately many fail to unlock throughout their entire lifetime. We all carry within us the breath of life from God. Most of the promises of God to us are based on the potentials that were embedded in the very fabric of our existence. God knows that we are capable of working out these promises into manifestation. The big elephant in the room is the essence of alignment. Whenever our humanity conforms to the standards set by divinity, there is an alignment that enable us tackle extraordinary goals.

Some people who may not necessarily be religious may attain this alignment by chance, in which case, they become inventors or superstars in an endeavor. Very few people have distinguished themselves as such so they are highly celebrated in society and many people wish but never get to become such. Divine alignment must not always be by chance because it can be learned and achieved by everyone who desires to function in this realm. "Blessed is the people that know the joyful sound: they shall walk, O LORD, in the light of thy countenance. In thy name shall they rejoice all the day: and in thy righteousness shall they be exalted. For thou art the glory of their strength: and in thy favour our horn shall be exalted" Psalms 89:15-17.

Divine alignment starts out with the ability to hear the sounds of heaven. For certain blessings to manifest in our lives, God, Cherubim, Man, Seraphim and Creation constitute five-spectrum entities that must all play a role. Whenever God speaks, the Cherubim immediately get compliant and execute the instruction. However, when such an instruction requires our participation in the process for manifestation, then it is essential that we hear the sound of His voice or at least become aware of what He has said that involves us. Our diligent response to this rhema-word automatically triggers Seraphim who are assigned to us and they act in compliance. The actions of Seraphim are what cause the works of creation to comply and glorify God.

GOD – CHERUBIM – MAN – SERAPHIM – CREATION

Essentially divinity is the realm where there must be a reverberation of the voice of God through Cherubim to Man then to Seraphim and ultimately Creation responds to the glory of God. Miraculous manifestations take place when man plays his proper role in the loop of divinity. Jesus taught the disciples how to become a part of the divinity loop. "For verily I say unto you, That whosoever shall say unto this mountain, Be thou removed, and be thou cast into the sea; and shall not doubt in his heart, but shall believe that those things which he saith shall come to pass; he shall have whatsoever he saith" Mark 11:23.

The narrative here was a day when Jesus was hungry and saw a fig tree in the distance. He expected that there would be fruits on the tree to answer to His hunger, and so when there were no fruits on the tree, He commanded the tree to dry up to the root. The following day the disciples observed that the tree is dead and drew the attention of Jesus to it. Jesus tells them that they can do the same. The core to activating our divinity potentials is faith. When we eliminate the element of doubt, our faith can move mountains.

6. THE VEIL STOREHOUSE

"And it shall come to pass in the increase, that ye shall give the fifth part unto Pharaoh, and four parts shall be your own, for seed of the field, and for your food, and for them of your households, and for food for your little ones" Genesis 47:24.

Joseph establishes that twenty percent of all the increase from cultivating seed in Egypt is for the Pharaoh. Remember that during the seven years of abundance, Joseph invested into twenty percent of the harvest of the Egyptians. That onetime investment is now garnering a lifetime return for the Pharaoh. Through this investment Joseph established the framework for the Pharaoh's absolute dominion over Egypt. Every Egyptian had to live their lives for the pleasure of the Pharaoh. Egyptian history reveals their belief in the relationship between their Pharaoh's and the cosmic world and the extension of their dominion to the afterlife. Such evidence is preserved by the alignment of their famous pyramids with cosmic bodies as well as the practice of mummification of their kings.

Dominion is both physical and spiritual. At the Table of Showbread Storehouse we establish ourselves in physical dominion over some specific territory. However, when we progress to function in the framework of the Altar of Incense Storehouse, it is the beginning of our quest for spiritual dominion. Spiritual dominion is how we leverage divine power over the cosmic world that comprises the kingdom of darkness. The kingdom of darkness gets particularly interested in anyone who attempts to bypass their control of the spiritual realm of this world. The Veil in the Tabernacle of Moses serves as the function of the ultimate barrier of the kingdom of darkness that is intended to stop our humanity from regaining the dominion we lost through Adam's fall. The Veil in the Tabernacle of Moses was made of four colors that speak to our divine potentials to overcome it. "And thou shalt make a vail of blue, and purple, and scarlet, and fine twined linen of cunning work: with cherubims shall it be made" Exodus 26:31.

1. Fine linen

This is the color that is significant of righteousness. We attain this color starting out at the Brazen Laver Storehouse were we are sanctified by the washing of water by the word of God and then as frankincense offered at the Altar of Incense. Jesus Christ is our righteousness and sanctification.

2. Scarlet

This is red color that is significant of redemption. We attain redemption starting out at the Altar of Sacrifice Storehouse through the blood of our Lord Jesus Christ and offered as onycha at the Altar of Incense. Jesus Christ is our redemption.

3. Blue

This is the color that is significant of Sonship. We attain sonship starting at the Lamp-stand Storehouse where Jesus Christ the Son of God brings us into sonship through the ministry of the Holy Spirit in our lives. Our sonship in Christ is represented by stacte offered at the Altar of Incense.

4. Purple

This is the color of royalty. We attain royalty at the Table of Showbread Storehouse where Jesus Christ the King of Kings has made us kings to reign with Him. Our royalty is expressed by galbanum offered up at the Altar of Incense.

The Veil was opened once a year on the Day of Atonement when the High Priest would sprinkle blood on the Veil. The High Priest would take some of the burning spices from the Altar of Incense and place it in a censor so that with the fumes of the incense serving as worship, the curtain was opened so he could enter the Most Holy Place in the tabernacle. "Jesus, when he had cried again with a loud voice, yielded up the ghost. And, behold, the veil of the temple was rent in twain from the top to the bottom; and the earth did quake, and the rocks rent; And the graves were opened; and many bodies of the saints which slept arose" Matthew 27:50-52.

Significantly, when Jesus Christ offered up himself on Calvary Cross, the veil in the temple was supernaturally torn in two and the Most Holy Place exposed to indicate that the sacrifice of His life was accepted as access for everyone to experience God's glory. "Having therefore, brethren, boldness to enter into the holiest by the blood of Jesus, By a new and living way, which he hath consecrated for us, through the veil, that is to say, his flesh; And having an high priest over the house of God; Let us draw near with a true heart in full assurance of faith, having our hearts sprinkled from an evil conscience, and our bodies washed with pure water. Let us hold fast the profession of our faith without wavering; (for he is faithful that promised" Hebrews 10:19-23.

- **Godly Dominion**

"And God said, Let us make man in our image, after our likeness: and let them have dominion over the fish of the sea, and over the fowl of the air, and over the cattle, and over all the earth, and over every creeping thing that creepeth upon the earth. So God created man in his own image, in the image of God created he him; male and female created he them. And God blessed them, and God said unto them, Be fruitful, and multiply, and replenish the earth, and subdue it: and have dominion over the fish of the sea, and over the fowl of the air, and over every living thing that moveth upon the earth. And God said, Behold, I have given you every herb bearing seed, which is upon the face of all the earth, and every tree, in the which is the fruit of a tree yielding seed; to you it shall be for meat. And to every beast of the earth, and to every fowl of the air, and to every thing that creepeth upon the earth, wherein there is life, I have given every green herb for meat: and it was so. And God saw every thing that he had made, and, behold, it was very good. And the evening and the morning were the sixth day" Genesis 1:26-31.

The decision to make man in God's own image and likeness tells a lot about how man must function in relationship to the entirety of creation. The entire earth and all vegetation and animals are placed at the feet of man. There is a clear sense of responsibility to leverage the mandate of dominion to harness the potentials of God's creation. This all-reaching mandate of dominion is fundamental to why the devil plotted the scheme of deception and stole it from Adam. The devil must have felt really threatened by the enormous scope of the blessing of dominion conferred upon man then and even now in the light of our potential restoration through Jesus Christ.

Water, Land, Vegetation, the Constellations, and Animals were all created to serve God's purpose in mankind. Throughout the scriptures we find out that these material forms of God's creation are all tokens of who we are potentially. To subdue creation physically, you would have to subdue them within the region of the human mind. Our far reaching advancements in science, economics, art, agriculture and other disciplines are all evidence of the exercise of the human mind. As humans we did not settle for the mediocrity of subsistence living, but have stretched our imagination to innovate and develop whatever we were inspired to achieve. This is the reason we are driving cars, flying in aircrafts and not riding just horses as a means of transportation.

- **The Fear of Mission**

Whenever there is an idea or desire to create or accomplish something new, there is an instant stimulus of the fear of failure in the human mind. This is a well orchestrated projection of the kingdom of darkness to challenge our quest to establish ourselves in dominion. Innovations always begin when we primarily conquer our own inhibitions. Every accomplished inventor endeavors first to overcome failure within them over and over again. This victory in the mind is the sustaining grace by which an innovator continues with an experiment until the desired outcome is achieved.

Having observed the scientific way by which the mind functions to overcome inhibitions, we have developed the disciplines of philosophy and psychology to help ourselves become masters of our world. While this is a stretching of the intellect to our advantage, it leaves out so many people trapped within the limitations of where we have reached with innovation. This gap remains the playground of the devil who will continue to prey upon our ignorance and destroy many.

- **Domineering, Manipulation And Controlling Spirits**

We cannot afford to eliminate God in our quest for true dominion. True dominion comes from God. It is how we overcome the opposition of the kingdom of darkness to our divinity in Christ. The advancement of the human intellect in philosophy and psychology means that we now not only know how to stimulate our minds to overcome inherent inhibitions, but also have developed sophisticated ways of domineering, manipulating and controlling our fellow man. While the positive use of the intellect is laudable, the vices are clearly inspired by the demonic. Without the God factor, most of our innovations simply feed into the agenda of the kingdom of darkness expanding their dominion over mankind. The devil inspires man with ideas for machinations to manipulate one another and no longer needs to use a serpent to do his dirty work. This way the devil keeps eating our lunch, while we pick up the tabs as humans!

The God-factor in dominion is how we persevere with a kingdom objective while maintaining the heartbeat of human benefit in all our endeavors. The kingdom of darkness keeps on its radar every activity on earth that attempt to bypass the confines of humanity. Demonic entities are assigned to oppose any human endeavors that could significantly dismantle the devil's agenda for this earth.

There are human collaborators who work with demonic entities to oppose all Christ-centered objectives on earth. Here in North America, there are occult centers in almost every community. Occultists are usually involved in our everyday lives with some serving in politics, law enforcement, banking and every other industry. With representation in every aspect of our civic existence, the kingdom of darkness has a very formidable potential for opposing Christ-centered kingdom objectives not only in the spiritual realm but also in the physical realm.

- **Corporate Greed, Oppression and Injustice**

The fall of Adam and Even in the Garden of Eden predicated the curse of enmity between the seed of man and that of the serpent. Instead of peaceful coexistence with one another, all living entities became either predator or prey. We find the predator and prey mindset playing out within all circles of human endeavor. Governments, corporations, organizations and individuals incline themselves either as predator or prey as fundamental motivation for endeavoring. Greed, oppression and injustice are core to the instincts of a predator. Unfortunately in our world today, people who are able to amass riches whether by fair or foul means are celebrated to a high degree, while it is considered almost a crime not to be rich. It is only natural that anyone who wants to break out of the trappings of mediocrity would pan towards a predator mindset.

It is no secret that you could eventually lose your job if as an individual, your core values incline you to resist being a predator in an organization with a predator mindset. Some corporations hire psychologists to pump up their human resource to master the vices of greed, oppression and injustice. In some organizations, the better you are at effectively

181

administering greed, oppression and injustice, the faster you rise up the corporate ladder. When you travel especially by rail throughout North America, you see dilapidated and abandoned communities which are mostly the consequences of corporate greed, oppression and injustice. Today businesses are all about higher margins and so the profit factor is not enough to keep the branches of a business open. If the margins of profit are not very high as comparing to other branches of a business, a branch is closed down and the employees are laid off.

Regardless of how long and how well you have served in an organization, the predator instinct axes you without recourse, the moment the appetite for greed cannot be gratified through your services. The devil must feel very gratified, watching greedy humans pick up the tabs while he eats their lunch! As long as we eliminate the God-factor from our quest for dominion, the devil will continue to reign through the very predator systems that underline our endeavors.

There is a sad statistic here in North America where several African American males especially are incarcerated because injustice is meted to them as suspects in crime cases. Instead of prosecutors doing a thorough investigation to get to the bottom of a case, many seek short cuts to quickly dispense with cases. Documents are forged as evidence, witnesses are coerced to make false statements and victims are sometimes threatened and forced to accept a deal of injustice. As a result some of those who are incarcerated and languish in prisons are often victims of human oppression within a supposed justice system. Ultimately the consequence for greed, oppression and injustice always leave us without a legacy for the next generation.

- **Dominion Wrestle**

"For the LORD hath redeemed Jacob, and ransomed him from the hand of him that was stronger than he. Therefore they shall come and sing in the height of Zion, and shall flow together to the goodness of the LORD, for wheat, and for wine, and for oil, and for the young of the flock and of the herd: and their soul shall be as a watered garden; and they shall not sorrow any more at all. Then shall the virgin rejoice in the dance, both young men and old together: for I will turn their mourning into joy, and will comfort them, and make them rejoice from their sorrow" Jeremiah 31:11-13.

The time frame for this prophetic scripture is several generations after the era of the patriarch Jacob. Jacob is mentioned as reference to the nation Israel because the nation is suffering from a condition of lost dominion. In the earlier phase of Jacob's life, he struggled with his twin brother Esau in a fight for dominion. Let us take a look at the six ways Jacob secured dominion in life.

Promise

It all begun while Jacob and Esau were still in the womb of Rebecca their mother. Rebecca was overwhelmed with the constant tussle of the unborn babies she was pregnant with and so she sought God.

"And the LORD said unto her, Two nations are in thy womb, and two manner of people shall be separated from thy bowels; and the one people shall be stronger than the other people; and the elder shall serve the younger" Genesis 25:23. The twins in Rebecca's womb was God's solution to an ancestral crises created by Abraham's relations with Hagar which resulted in the birth of Ishmael. Biologically Ishmael was Abraham's firstborn son so he should have inherited the legacy of Abraham. However, Ishmael was not the design of God and His birth was predicated by the anxiety to have a biological progeny. At some point, Hagar and Ishmael were sent away so Ishmael did not inherit Abraham's blessings. Though Isaac inherited Abraham's blessings and became heir of the spiritual heritage promised by God, the spirit of Ishmael remained in contest for this same blessing. This contest for dominion is the reason the fetus in Rebecca was split and those two babies represent the heritage of Ishmael as Esau and Isaac as Jacob.

"For it is written, that Abraham had two sons, the one by a bondmaid, the other by a freewoman. But he who was of the bondwoman was born after the flesh; but he of the freewoman was by promise. Which things are an allegory: for these are the two covenants; the one from the mount Sinai, which gendereth to bondage, which is Agar. For this Agar is mount Sinai in Arabia, and answereth to Jerusalem which now is, and is in bondage with her children. But Jerusalem which is above is free, which is the mother of us all. For it is written, Rejoice, thou barren that bearest not; break forth and cry, thou that travailest not: for the desolate hath many more children than she which hath an husband. Now we, brethren, as Isaac was, are the children of promise. But as then he that was born after the flesh persecuted him that was born after the Spirit, even so it is now. Nevertheless what saith the scripture? Cast out the bondwoman and her son: for the son of the bondwoman shall not be heir with the son of the freewoman. So then, brethren, we are not children of the bondwoman, but of the free" Galatians 4:22-31.

Dominion is essentially the fight between flesh and Spirit which continues to plague us today in our walk with God. Like the condition in Rebecca's womb which was the initial battle field for dominion between Esau and Jacob, we all have the burden to overcome the flesh by walking in the Spirit. We have to win the wrestle for dominion within us in the spiritual realm. Our Christian lives must be predicated by faith in the leading of the Holy Spirit. The promises of God for our lives are the first key to dominion.

Procurement

Though Esau came out first and so was the firstborn, the scripture shows that Jacob held on to the heels of Esau as they came out of the birth canal. This led those who were present at their birth to name this second twin as a 'supplanter'. Esau becomes a skillful hunter early in life. He is very successful at bringing home animal trappings and his father Isaac loves the venison. Jacob on the hand does not display phenomenal traits and was most likely 'the invisible one in the room.' While the state of mediocrity may push some people into a mediocre mindset all their lives, others seek out how to overcome their mediocrity. This is why Jacob endeavored to seek the root to his condition and his mother Rebecca would have told him of the revelation she had received about their divine destiny.

Through this revelation, Jacob knows that dominion belongs to him by divine design but the question is: how? This is when he discovers the root of Esau's phenomenal success, which is the firstborn status. In the light of this discovery, it becomes Jacob's burden to seek the firstborn blessing, so on the day Esau seeks food from him, the only need worthy of the exchange is Esau's birthright. Jacob requests that Esau trade-in his firstborn status for the pot of red stew. Every believer has access to firstborn status through honoring the covenant of tithing. Firstborn status through tithing is the second key to dominion.

Diligence

When Isaac realized that he was nearing his death, he intended to pass on the legacy of blessings to his progeny. Though Isaac was aware that Esau had sold his birthright to Jacob, he told Esau to bring him venison so he could bless Esau. When Rebecca learns of this, she plots with Jacob to go and get the blessings instead. At this point Isaac has a sight impediment so Jacob is able to receive the blessing. This blessing from Isaac to Jacob is the ancestral legacy that was passed on from Abraham to Isaac. Throughout his life to this point, Esau has demonstrated a lifestyle that is contrary to this legacy and crowned it by marrying a wife from the heathen neighbors.

Dominion thrives on values that are core to a particular heritage and clearly Jacob had demonstrated through his character that he was upholding the values of Abraham that God sought to perpetuate in that lineage. Today, God gives every believer the opportunity to receive a spiritual, emotional and financial legacy from specific people. If we apply ourselves to learn from such spiritual fathers and apply ourselves to these values, we receive the legacy of dominion. You will notice that after receiving Isaac's legacy, Jacob is prompted by his parents to run away from Esau to Haran. On this journey Jacob encounters God at Bethel where God ratifies the covenant with Abraham and Isaac with Jacob. Jacob received the seal of God's approval. When we learn and serve diligently those who God has placed over us as mentors, we receive the seal of God's approval for legitimacy of dominion. Diligence with legacy is the third key to dominion.

Purpose

Jacob arrives in Haran and meets up with his uncle Laban. Jacob works fourteen years rearing the sheep of Laban as dowry for Leah and Rachael who became his wives. At some point, Jacob decides to move away from Laban to establish himself but then Laban cuts a deal with him so that Jacob would continue serving Laban. The reason Laban proposes this deal is that he has observed that there is an unusual blessing upon Jacob that has translated into phenomenal increase of his flocks over which Jacob is in charge. Jacob agrees to this deal but then Laban gets treacherous and keeps changing the terms of the agreement to accommodate his greed. God intervenes to spare Jacob the heartache of injustice by revealing to Jacob how to increase his flock in the face of Laban's oppression. For the first time, Jacob experiences his dominion in action. Through divine inspiration Jacob becomes exceeding prosperous in his work as a shepherd. If we are true to the vocation of our divine destiny, we would receive divine inspiration to advance regardless of the schemes of the enemy. Servitude in divine purpose is the fourth key to dominion.

Escape

In the light of Laban's growing jealousy, God instructs Jacob to move away from Laban without giving notice. This is not the conventional way of departing from one's family relatives but Jacob mobilizes his family and build-up of riches and then secretly elopes. When Laban discovers this, he pursues after Jacob. While in pursuit, God intervenes and warns Laban not to hurt Jacob or curse him. The blessing of Jacob's God-given dominion protected him in an unusual way. Obedience to unconventional divine instructions is the fifth key to how God preserves us in dominion.

Wrestle

The vicious encounter with Laban came to an end and Jacob proceeded on his journey. He is going through Esau's territory and so he sends a gift of appeasement to his twin brother. Esau is not amused and mobilizes an army of soldiers to confront Jacob. When Jacob learns that Esau was coming after him with an army, he is perplexed because he senses vengeance at hand from his brother. Jacob sought God all-night in prayer. "And Jacob was left alone; and there wrestled a man with him until the breaking of the day. And when he saw that he prevailed not against him, he touched the hollow of his thigh; and the hollow of Jacob's thigh was out of joint, as he wrestled with him. And he said, Let me go, for the day breaketh. And he said, I will not let thee go, except thou bless me. And he said unto him, What is thy name? And he said, Jacob. And he said, Thy name shall be called no more Jacob, but Israel: for as a prince hast thou power with God and with men, and hast prevailed" Genesis 32:24-28.

Jacob has been going through a cycle of struggles to maintain the blessing of dominion. This particular confrontation with Esau is unraveling and he feels it in his bones. He has to settle this once and for all and so he separates himself from his family and goes to seek God. While travailing in prayer, the experience turns into a physical encounter where he is engaged in an actual wrestle with an angel. The angel reveals the root of Jacob's challenges as the misnaming at his birth. He was wrongly named Jacob when he should have been called Israel. The name Israel means that, as a prince, he has power with God and with man. In the morning when Jacob met with Esau, the encounter which could have turned out as a bloody exchange ended up as a peaceful encounter between the twin brothers. 'Power with God and power with man' is the full meaning of dominion. Travailing prayer is the sixth and final key to dominion.

7. THE ARK OF THE COVENANT STOREHOUSE

"And they said, Thou hast saved our lives: let us find grace in the sight of my lord, and we will be Pharaoh's servants" Genesis 47:25. If we should paraphrase this statement of the Egyptians within the context of the narrative, it would say: "Joseph, you have been merciful to us in ameliorating our condition, we want to remain in this favor so we shall endeavor to serve the Pharaoh all our lives."

The key word here is 'mercy' and the Egyptians are imploring Joseph to remain in that framework with the Pharaoh. Mercy simply means 'change' and is always used in the environment of judgment. The cycle of seven years of abundance followed by seven years of famine has come to an end. Egypt has changed dramatically during this fourteen year period. The people as well as their land assets all belong to the Pharaoh who now wields unlimited authority. The Egyptians have expressed to Joseph, their desire to remain in the framework of the Pharaoh's mercies.

- **Mercy Prerogative**

It is common for parents to advise their children that good education and hard-work translates into financial success. While good education and hard-work are important components of financial success, many people who have upheld these values in our world today, have ended up disenfranchised, indebted and disinherited due to a rigged financial system. Financial institutions such as banks, securities investment companies, mortgage companies and insurance companies have devised ways of robbing us of our hard earned resources. All over the world, financial securities exchanges function almost like a casino by engaging in legalized gambling of people's investments. As a result of these unscrupulous schemes, many who work in these financial institutions have amassed great riches while many innocent people have lost their investments, homes and entitlements.

The Ark of the Covenant, which was the object of divine judgment in the tabernacle of Moses, was situated in the Most Holy Place. It was designed to incorporate a box that contained the Ten Commandments, two Cherubim and a mercy seat. These three components of the Ark of the Covenant reveal the fundamentals of divine judgment. The High Priest entered this Most Holy Place once a year to receive God's judgment on behalf of the Israelites. Similarly every human being has the opportunity to experience divine judgment once a year. Divine judgment gives everyone a chance to experience divine justice. God has established a mercy-centered calendar for all humans through the seven-day creation cycle of Sabbath rest, seventh-year release, and fiftieth year restoration jubilee. Divine judgment facilitates us with the prerogative of mercy such that everyone can have the chance of divine privileges to advance in life.

1. The Box Containing The Ten Commandments

The Ten Commandments that was engraved on stone was placed in the box of the Ark of the Covenant. This box was the base of the Ark and signified the logos-word of God. How we conduct ourselves in obedience to the principles set forth in the scriptures is the first factor of divine judgment.

Overcome Disenfranchisement By The Sabbath Rest

For six days, God created and made the heavens, the earth and its inhabitants. However on the seventh day, God rested. He sanctified the seventh day and blessed it. The seventh day is significant of how we enter into God's rest. He commanded the Israelites to rest from their works as well as their beasts of burden. Rest allows every human and animal to recuperate. It is in an act of mercy to our human body as well as to the horses that carry us in transportation and the ox that plow our fields. The Sabbath is significant of how we leverage faith in God's word and partake in His holiness and authority.

Holiness: In practice, it is impossible to be in absolute compliance with the entire logos-word of God and so in the season of divine judgment, God throws everyone a life-line.

"Furthermore we have had fathers of our flesh which corrected us, and we gave them reverence: shall we not much rather be in subjection unto the Father of spirits, and live? For they verily for a few days chastened us after their own pleasure; but he for our profit, that we might be partakers of his holiness. Now no chastening for the present seemeth to be joyous, but grievous: nevertheless afterward it yieldeth the peaceable fruit of righteousness unto them which are exercised thereby. Wherefore lift up the hands which hang down, and the feeble knees; And make straight paths for your feet, lest that which is lame be turned out of the way; but let it rather be healed. Follow peace with all men, and holiness, without which no man shall see the Lord" Hebrews 12:9-14. In the season of divine judgment, God initiates the process of bringing us into His Rest by throwing us a life-line of His holiness in those areas where we are severely disenfranchised. Without holiness no one can experience God's abiding presence of divine rest. Every area of our lives where we fail to experience the victory of the covenant promises of God is a reflection of our disenfranchisement. Salvation in Christ Jesus ushers us into spiritual citizenship with Israel (Ephesians 2).

We become partakers of the blessings of Abraham through the sacrifice on the cross of Jesus Christ. Any requirement of the covenant that we become guilty of becomes the basis of our disenfranchisement. Just as a citizen of any country that violates its laws become guilty and may be incarcerated and denied their basic rights of freedom, we may be denied of our covenant rights as citizens of God's kingdom when we violate provisions of the covenant. However as an act of mercy, God throws everyone who seeks His mercies, a life-line of His holiness in those areas we are disenfranchised and seek His mercies. He convicts us with an inspired logos-word so that we can partake in His holiness. The logos-word is like water that washes us and makes us clean. We become sanctified by our resolution to walk in this word. This is how we step out of the guilty charge that was basis for our disenfranchisement. When we comply with the inspiration of the logos-word, we are discharged from the accusations and sentence of disenfranchisement. Furthermore mercy is a 'give and take' blessing so it is important that we share our convictions from the logos-word with others. Witnessing to others with the logos-word that has convicted us is our act of mercy that completes the cycle of mercy.

Authority: This is the next blessing of mercy. In any aspect of life where we partake of God's holiness, we also share in divine authority. Authority means 'delegated power'. It is how we legitimately control the spiritual world of angels and devils. Angels may have become dormant or confused by our careless words for which reason they are unsure of what to do for us and devils may have kept us in spiritual prison using our past sins as their mandate. When we step into the life-line of holiness, we have to deploy our authority in blood of Jesus. Jesus said in Matthew 16:19 - "And I will give unto thee the keys of the kingdom of heaven: and whatsoever thou shalt bind on earth shall be bound in heaven: and whatsoever thou shalt loose on earth shall be loosed in heaven."

The keys of the kingdom give us the right to permit angelic activity or disallow demonic activity. By unleashing the divine authority of the blood of Jesus Christ we mandate angels to foster positive changes and break the hold of devils over our freedoms. In any aspect of life where we partake of God's holiness, we are also refranchised with our divine authority.

2. The Cherubim

The two Cherubim situated top of the box of the Ark of the Covenant signified the ministry of angels who flow from God's presence to reveal God's rhema-word to us. How we conduct ourselves in obedience to the rhema-word is the second factor of divine judgment.

Overcome Debt By The Seventh-Year Release

God instructed the Israelites to cultivate the fields for six years and leave the land to rest on the seventh. The land was to lay fallow in the seventh-year to recuperate. This practice is known to be of great agricultural prudence and so today many non-Jewish people observe it. During this seventh year which was also known as the year of release, all slaves of Israelite origin were set free and those who owed debts were released of their indebtedness (Deuteronomy 15). Freedom from bond-service and debt are acts of mercy which not only afford other people another chance in life but is significantly core to fulfilling our divine purpose and for building wealth.

Purpose: Everyone on planet earth has a divinely ordained purpose. Failure to pursue our divine purpose is the root of debt. Today the greatest cancer in the Western hemisphere is financial debt. Typical advice from financial professionals would be to work more jobs, change your career for a more lucrative job, spend less or subscribe to financial consolidation of your debts. While these solutions may offer some form of relief, the real root of debt which still lingers after all diligence is done is the failure to fulfill divine purpose. Divine purpose is a basic seed God has endowed everyone with. This seed is the oil well resident in us. In 2 Kings 4, the story of the widow who came to Elisha because of her indebtedness and the threat that her sons would be taken into bond-service is a reflection of how we typically end up in debt. Elisha simply tells her to pour her oil into the vessels of her neighbors as the antidote to debt and bond-service. It is common knowledge that oil companies all over the world are usually very rich from that enterprise. Similarly those who have endeavored in the arena of their divine purpose contribute their quota to the advancement of society so they are well rewarded by their impact. God's Covenant resources flow in the direction of all those who function in the arena of their divine purpose.

Wealth: This is the next blessing of mercy. While purpose is how we sow the seed of our impact to society and may earn us some riches, wealth is how we consolidate ourselves in prosperity. "But thou shalt remember the LORD thy God: for it is he that giveth thee power to get wealth, that he may establish his covenant which he sware unto thy fathers, as it is this day" Deuteronomy 8:18. Wealth begins with acknowledging God as our source. When we fulfill our part of His covenant through tithing, He preserves our riches so they translate into wealth. God gives us the revelation of wisdom to build various systems that consolidate us in wealth. There is a unique way for everyone to become entrenched in wealth and so it is important that we pay attention to the divine revelation that comes to us as a benefit of tithing. Though others may find investment into stocks their way of building wealth, you may receive an inspiration to build orphanages across the world. Real wealth is spiritual and is associated with royalty. It is a domain where the riches of this world answer to you without question because God has sanctioned it. Wealth is a blessing from God that positions you in a loop of helping the needy, providing for those who are engaged in Ministry, humanitarian missions and fostering strategic changes in society.

3. The Mercy Seat

Situated on top of the box and in between the two Cherubim was a mercy seat. The mercy seat was where God sat to dispense judgment. Mercy is the third factor of divine judgment.

While obedience to the logos-word and the rhema-word are core to divine judgment, how we have dispensed mercy to others is the most important factor of divine judgment. "For whosoever shall keep the whole law, and yet offend in one point, he is guilty of all. For he that said, Do not commit adultery, said also, Do not kill. Now if thou commit no adultery, yet if thou kill, thou art become a transgressor of the law. So speak ye, and so do, as they that shall be judged by the law of liberty. For he shall have judgment without mercy, that hath shewed no mercy; and mercy rejoiceth against judgment" James 2:10-13.

Mercy is a prerogative of the human heart and so ignorance of the logos-word or inability to obey the rhema-word owing to circumstances beyond our control does not excuse anyone from divine judgment. While it is humanly impossible to be fully compliant with every logo-word and rhema-word, we are all wired with the natural ability to exercise compassion and so even without a relationship with God, we are subject to judgment based upon how we have dispensed mercy to others. Jesus puts it this way in the beatitudes: "Blessed are the merciful: for they shall obtain mercy" Matthew 5:7.

Within every human is the potential to foster change in another man's condition of life. Though we may all have unique circumstances that beset us, we all have various abilities and resources by which we can alter the challenges of one another. If we become trapped by self-centeredness and hold back these abilities and resources from those who require them, then we are unmerciful and risk being judged by the same standard. Our level of dispensing mercy determines the level of mercy we experience in life.

Overcome Disinheritance by the Fiftieth-Year Restoration Jubilee

After seven cycles of release are completed, the trumpet of the jubilee was to be sounded in the fiftieth year. This sound was announcement for the restoration of land. Israelites were not to sell their lands permanently to others because it was given to them as their divine inheritance. The potential within the land allocated to each Israelite tribe reflected their divine destiny. Over time however some Israelites became victims of unfortunate conditions that made them lease their lands. During the Jubilee, every such transaction was automatically terminated and land was restored to their legitimate owners. The Jubilee afforded every Israelite the opportunity to return to their God-given place of destiny. The Jubilee mandate was the divine provision of mercy by which all Israelites experienced divine restoration. We tap into this covenant privilege by reverence, counsel and might.

Reverence: The domain of our inheritance in Christ is primarily spiritual and then physical. After the resurrection, the disciples asked Jesus about the timing for the restoration of Israel's national heritage.

At this point Israel was under Roman colonization so it was a natural burden of the Israelites to be restored with their dominion as a nation. The response of Jesus is interesting:

"When they therefore were come together, they asked of him, saying, Lord, wilt thou at this time restore again the kingdom to Israel? And he said unto them, It is not for you to know the times or the seasons, which the Father hath put in his own power. But ye shall receive power, after that the Holy Ghost is come upon you: and ye shall be witnesses unto me both in Jerusalem, and in all Judaea, and in Samaria, and unto the uttermost part of the earth." Jesus makes what I will refer to as one of the most significant announcements about one of the victories of the cross of His crucifixion. The land territory of Israel no longer defines the boundaries of God's kingdom on earth. This is the end of the era where ownership of physical land alone is tantamount to dominion and the beginning of virtual reality. Jesus tells the disciples that they would be empowered supernaturally by the Holy Ghost so that they can impact the whole world.

"Wherefore we receiving a kingdom which cannot be moved, let us have grace, whereby we may serve God acceptably with reverence and godly fear" Hebrews 12:28. An important key to our spiritual kingdom is reverence for God. Reverence means the fear, honor or respect of God. We are in the era of God's kingdom where He himself is allocating territory to those who revere Him. People who are disorderly, disobedient and stubborn in heart do not reverence God and so cannot find a place of dominion. Notice that in the scripture above, God furnishes us with grace, which is the divine ability to serve Him with reverence. Furthermore we must reverence those who God places in leadership at home, work, Church, the community and in government so that the cycle of mercy is complete.

Counsel: This is the next blessing of mercy. Counsel is divinely ordained help. Here the Holy Spirit who is our chief counselor assigns specific people to us either by revelation or contact opportunity. Such people find it in their hearts to become supportive of whatever is our divine purpose. They extend professional and material help to facilitate our endeavors. Furthermore they give us access to their world of friends and associations. This is how God enlarges our coast and increases our sphere of impact. "Without counsel purposes are disappointed: but in the multitude of counsellors they are established." Proverbs 15:22. Counsel is the conduit by which God streams divine wisdom that we may better appreciate from fellow humans. It is important never to ignore the exchange rule of mercy. Those who avail themselves as conduits for the expansion of your domain need to be reciprocated. You must avail yourself to provide help in their time of need.

Might: This is the last blessing of mercy. 'Might' means 'power in action'. As human beings we are loaded with so much divine potentials that only few people unleash the full capacity during their lifetime. Worst of all, most people live in ignorance of such potentials. The Apostle Paul puts it this way in his letter to the Ephesians;

"For this cause I bow my knees unto the Father of our Lord Jesus Christ, Of whom the whole family in heaven and earth is named, That he would grant you, according to the riches of his glory, to be strengthened with might by his Spirit in the inner man; That Christ may dwell in your hearts by faith; that ye, being rooted and grounded in love, May be able to comprehend with all saints what is the breadth, and length, and depth, and height; And to know the love of Christ, which passeth knowledge, that ye might be filled with all the fulness of God. Now unto him that is able to do exceeding abundantly above all that we ask or think, according to the power that worketh in us, Unto him be glory in the church by Christ Jesus throughout all ages, world without end. Amen" Ephesians 3:14-21.

Knowledge of the potentials resident in us as humans is the beginning of might. At every point in time there is a measure of divine power that is made available to us. Remember that we started out in this dimension of mercy by accepting the life-line of participating in God's holiness, then leveraging divine authority, then functioning in divine purpose, building wealth, subscribing to a culture of reverence and working with counsel. These six prerogatives set the stage for the might of God. To the degree that we plunge ourselves into holiness defines our scope of divine authority, purpose, wealth, reverence, counsel and ultimately might. Might therefore is a buildup of intuitive knowledge of God. It is our real spiritual capacity to deploy the abilities of God within us. Might is the manifestation of God's glory from within us. It is the heavy-weightiness of God that exemplifies our leadership capabilities and impact attributes. Joseph demonstrated such might as Prime Minister of Egypt and his global impact is an everlasting testimony.

REFERENCES

Wilmington's Guide to the Bible by Dr. Harold   L. Wilmington

Hebrew-Greek Keyword Study Bible by Spiros Zhodiates

Online Encyclopedia – www.wikipedia.org

Manifestation Plan

Manifestation Plan

Manifestation Plan

www.ingramcontent.com/pod-product-compliance
Lightning Source LLC
Chambersburg PA
CBHW071950090426
42740CB00011B/1888